**Data Communicatio**
**Complete Self-Asse**



The guidance in this Self-A... best practices and standards in business process architecture, design and quality management. The guidance is also based on the professional judgment of the individual collaborators listed in the Acknowledgments.


http://theartofservice.com
service@theartofservice.com

# Table of Contents

# About The Art of Service

The Art of Service, Business Process Architects since 2000, is dedicated to helping stakeholders achieve excellence.

Defining, designing, creating, and implementing a process to solve a stakeholders challenge or meet an objective is the most valuable role... In EVERY group, company, organization and department.

Unless you're talking a one-time, single-use project, there should be a process. Whether that process is managed and implemented by humans, AI, or a combination of the two, it needs to be designed by someone with a complex enough perspective to ask the right questions.

Someone capable of asking the right questions and step back and say, 'What are we really trying to accomplish here? And is there a different way to look at it?'

With The Art of Service's Standard Requirements Self-Assessments, we empower people who can do just that — whether their title is marketer, entrepreneur, manager, salesperson, consultant, Business Process Manager, executive assistant, IT Manager, CIO etc... —they are the people who rule the future. They are people who watch the process as it happens, and ask the right questions to make the process work better.

**Contact us when you need any support with this Self-Assessment and any help with templates, blue-prints and examples of standard documents you might need:**

http://theartofservice.com
service@theartofservice.com

# Included Resources - how to access

**Included with your purchase of the book is the Data**

**Communication Self-Assessment Spreadsheet Dashboard which contains all questions and Self-Assessment areas and auto-generates insights, graphs, and project RACI planning - all with examples to get you started right away.**

How? Simply send an email to
**access@theartofservice.com**
with this books' title in the subject to get the Data Communication Self Assessment Tool right away.

You will receive the following contents with New and Updated specific criteria:

- The latest quick edition of the book in PDF
- The latest complete edition of the book in PDF, which criteria correspond to the criteria in...
- The Self-Assessment Excel Dashboard, and...
- Example pre-filled Self-Assessment Excel Dashboard to get familiar with results generation
- In-depth specific Checklists covering the topic
- Project management checklists and templates to assist with implementation

**INCLUDES LIFETIME SELF ASSESSMENT UPDATES**

Every self assessment comes with Lifetime Updates and Lifetime Free Updated Books. Lifetime Updates is an industry-first feature which allows you to receive verified self assessment updates, ensuring you always have the most accurate information at your fingertips.

Get it now- you will be glad you did - do it now, before you forget.

Send an email to **access@theartofservice.com** with this books' title in the subject to get the Data Communication Self Assessment Tool right away.

# Purpose of this Self-Assessment

This Self-Assessment has been developed to improve understanding of the requirements and elements of Data Communication, based on best practices and standards in business process architecture, design and quality management.

It is designed to allow for a rapid Self-Assessment to determine how closely existing management practices and procedures correspond to the elements of the Self-Assessment.

The criteria of requirements and elements of Data Communication have been rephrased in the format of a Self-Assessment questionnaire, with a seven-criterion scoring system, as explained in this document.

In this format, even with limited background knowledge of Data Communication, a manager can quickly review existing operations to determine how they measure up to the standards. This in turn can serve as the starting point of a 'gap analysis' to identify management tools or system elements that might usefully be implemented in the organization to help improve overall performance.

# How to use the Self-Assessment

On the following pages are a series of questions to identify to what extent your Data Communication initiative is complete in comparison to the requirements set in standards.

To facilitate answering the questions, there is a space in front of each question to enter a score on a scale of '1' to '5'.

1 Strongly Disagree

2 Disagree

3 Neutral

4 Agree

5 Strongly Agree

*Read the question and rate it with the following in front of mind:*

**'In my belief,
the answer to this question is clearly defined'.**

There are two ways in which you can choose to interpret this statement;

1. how aware are you that the answer to the question is clearly defined
2. for more in-depth analysis you can choose to gather evidence and confirm the answer to the question. This obviously will take more time, most Self-Assessment users opt for the first way to interpret the question and dig deeper later on based on the outcome of the overall Self-Assessment.

A score of '1' would mean that the answer is not clear at all, where a '5' would mean the answer is crystal clear and defined. Leave emtpy when the question is not applicable or you don't want to answer it, you can skip it without affecting your score. Write your score in the space provided.

After you have responded to all the appropriate statements in each section, compute your average score for that section, using the formula provided, and round to the nearest tenth. Then transfer to the corresponding spoke in the Data Communication Scorecard on the second next page of the Self-Assessment.

Your completed Data Communication Scorecard will give you a clear presentation of which Data Communication areas need attention.

# Data Communication Scorecard Example

Example of how the finalized Scorecard can look like:

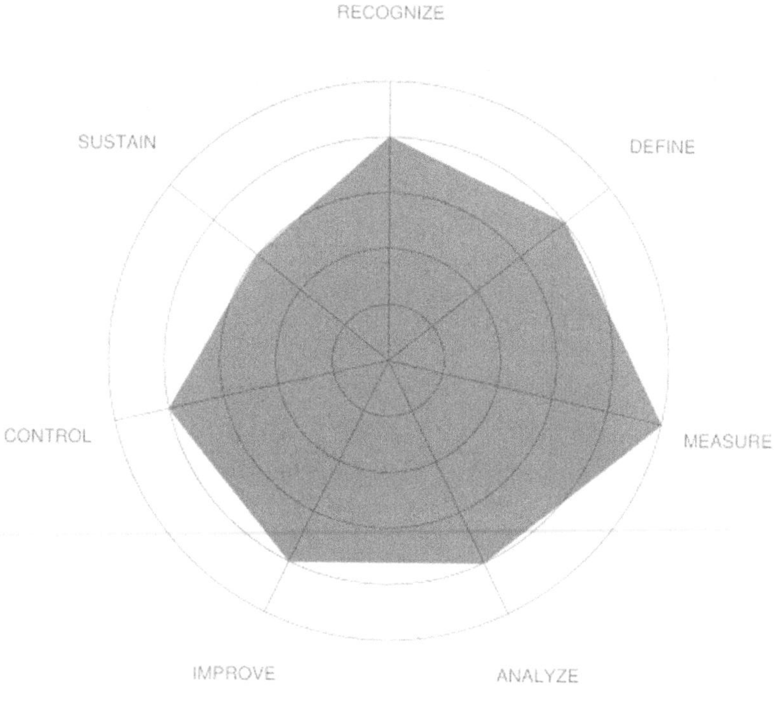

# Data Communication Scorecard

Your Scores:

# BEGINNING OF THE SELF-ASSESSMENT:

# CRITERION #1: RECOGNIZE

INTENT: Be aware of the need for change. Recognize that there is an unfavorable variation, problem or symptom.

In my belief, the answer to this question is clearly defined:

5 Strongly Agree

4 Agree

3 Neutral

2 Disagree

1 Strongly Disagree

1. What is the Data communication problem definition? What do you need to resolve?
<--- Score

2. Are employees recognized or rewarded for performance that demonstrates the highest levels of integrity?
<--- Score

<--- Score

23. What vendors make products that address the Data communication needs?
<--- Score

24. Who needs what information?
<--- Score

25. Whom do you really need or want to serve?
<--- Score

26. What else needs to be measured?
<--- Score

27. What are the clients issues and concerns?
<--- Score

28. Who defines the rules in relation to any given issue?
<--- Score

29. Who should resolve the Data communication issues?
<--- Score

30. How does it fit into your organizational needs and tasks?
<--- Score

31. Do you need different information or graphics?
<--- Score

32. How much are sponsors, customers, partners, stakeholders involved in Data communication? In other words, what are the risks, if Data

communication does not deliver successfully?
<--- Score

33. What training and capacity building actions are needed to implement proposed reforms?
<--- Score

34. What are the timeframes required to resolve each of the issues/problems?
<--- Score

35. Will Data communication deliverables need to be tested and, if so, by whom?
<--- Score

36. When a Data communication manager recognizes a problem, what options are available?
<--- Score

37. What situation(s) led to this Data communication Self Assessment?
<--- Score

38. Do you need to avoid or amend any Data communication activities?
<--- Score

39. What is the problem and/or vulnerability?
<--- Score

40. Who needs budgets?
<--- Score

41. Does Data communication create potential expectations in other areas that need to be recognized and considered?

<--- Score

42. How can auditing be a preventative security measure?
<--- Score

43. What information do users need?
<--- Score

44. As a sponsor, customer or management, how important is it to meet goals, objectives?
<--- Score

45. What are your needs in relation to Data communication skills, labor, equipment, and markets?
<--- Score

46. What prevents you from making the changes you know will make you a more effective Data communication leader?
<--- Score

47. To what extent does each concerned units management team recognize Data communication as an effective investment?
<--- Score

48. Do you recognize Data communication achievements?
<--- Score

49. What tools and technologies are needed for a custom Data communication project?
<--- Score

50. Are employees recognized for desired behaviors?

<--- Score

51. Is it needed?
<--- Score

52. What Data communication coordination do you need?
<--- Score

53. What are the minority interests and what amount of minority interests can be recognized?
<--- Score

54. Are your goals realistic? Do you need to redefine your problem? Perhaps the problem has changed or maybe you have reached your goal and need to set a new one?
<--- Score

55. Why is this needed?
<--- Score

56. Consider your own Data communication project, what types of organizational problems do you think might be causing or affecting your problem, based on the work done so far?
<--- Score

57. Who else hopes to benefit from it?
<--- Score

58. Is the quality assurance team identified?
<--- Score

59. What resources or support might you need?
<--- Score

60. Does the problem have ethical dimensions?
<--- Score

61. What do employees need in the short term?
<--- Score

62. How are the Data communication's objectives aligned to the group's overall stakeholder strategy?
<--- Score

63. Are you dealing with any of the same issues today as yesterday? What can you do about this?
<--- Score

64. What is the smallest subset of the problem you can usefully solve?
<--- Score

65. To what extent would your organization benefit from being recognized as a award recipient?
<--- Score

66. Are there Data communication problems defined?
<--- Score

67. Are there any specific expectations or concerns about the Data communication team, Data communication itself?
<--- Score

68. Where do you need to exercise leadership?
<--- Score

69. Think about the people you identified for your Data communication project and the project

responsibilities you would assign to them, what kind of training do you think they would need to perform these responsibilities effectively?
<--- Score

70. Are controls defined to recognize and contain problems?
<--- Score

71. Can management personnel recognize the monetary benefit of Data communication?
<--- Score

72. Will a response program recognize when a crisis occurs and provide some level of response?
<--- Score

73. Do you know what you need to know about Data communication?
<--- Score

74. What extra resources will you need?
<--- Score

75. Do you have/need 24-hour access to key personnel?
<--- Score

76. What problems are you facing and how do you consider Data communication will circumvent those obstacles?
<--- Score

77. Who are your key stakeholders who need to sign off?
<--- Score

78. Which needs are not included or involved?
<--- Score

79. Have you identified your Data communication key performance indicators?
<--- Score

80. How do you take a forward-looking perspective in identifying Data communication research related to market response and models?
<--- Score

81. What Data communication problem should be solved?
<--- Score

82. What are the Data communication resources needed?
<--- Score

83. How do you identify subcontractor relationships?
<--- Score

84. Will new equipment/products be required to facilitate Data communication delivery, for example is new software needed?
<--- Score

85. What would happen if Data communication weren't done?
<--- Score

86. How many trainings, in total, are needed?
<--- Score

87. How do you recognize an Data communication objection?
<--- Score

88. What does Data communication success mean to the stakeholders?
<--- Score

89. What do you need to start doing?
<--- Score

90. What needs to be done?
<--- Score

91. Who needs to know?
<--- Score

92. What is the recognized need?
<--- Score

93. Why the need?
<--- Score

94. Will it solve real problems?
<--- Score

95. What are the stakeholder objectives to be achieved with Data communication?
<--- Score

Add up total points for this section:
_____ = Total points for this section

Divided by: ______ (number of statements answered) = ______
Average score for this section

Transfer your score to the Data communication Index at the beginning of the Self-Assessment.

# CRITERION #2: DEFINE:

INTENT: Formulate the stakeholder problem. Define the problem, needs and objectives.

In my belief, the answer to this question is clearly defined:

5 Strongly Agree

4 Agree

3 Neutral

2 Disagree

1 Strongly Disagree

1. Will a Data communication production readiness review be required?
<--- Score

2. Is there a Data communication management charter, including stakeholder case, problem and goal statements, scope, milestones, roles and responsibilities, communication plan?
<--- Score

3. Who is gathering Data communication information?
<--- Score

4. How do you manage changes in Data communication requirements?
<--- Score

5. What are (control) requirements for Data communication Information?
<--- Score

6. How do you think the partners involved in Data communication would have defined success?
<--- Score

7. Are required metrics defined, what are they?
<--- Score

8. Is there a completed SIPOC representation, describing the Suppliers, Inputs, Process, Outputs, and Customers?
<--- Score

9. What specifically is the problem? Where does it occur? When does it occur? What is its extent?
<--- Score

10. What are the core elements of the Data communication business case?
<--- Score

11. What critical content must be communicated – who, what, when, where, and how?
<--- Score

12. How do you gather Data communication requirements?
<--- Score

13. Is there a clear Data communication case definition?
<--- Score

14. Is there a critical path to deliver Data communication results?
<--- Score

15. What is the scope of the Data communication work?
<--- Score

16. What are the compelling stakeholder reasons for embarking on Data communication?
<--- Score

17. What knowledge or experience is required?
<--- Score

18. Are task requirements clearly defined?
<--- Score

19. Is data collected and displayed to better understand customer(s) critical needs and requirements.
<--- Score

20. What Data communication requirements should be gathered?
<--- Score

21. What is the scope of the Data communication

effort?
<--- Score

22. Has a project plan, Gantt chart, or similar been developed/completed?
<--- Score

23. What is the context?
<--- Score

24. What are the dynamics of the communication plan?
<--- Score

25. How was the 'as is' process map developed, reviewed, verified and validated?
<--- Score

26. How would you define the culture at your organization, how susceptible is it to Data communication changes?
<--- Score

27. Are customer(s) identified and segmented according to their different needs and requirements?
<--- Score

28. If substitutes have been appointed, have they been briefed on the Data communication goals and received regular communications as to the progress to date?
<--- Score

29. How do you hand over Data communication context?
<--- Score

30. Have specific policy objectives been defined?
<--- Score

31. What is in the scope and what is not in scope?
<--- Score

32. What is a worst-case scenario for losses?
<--- Score

33. How are consistent Data communication definitions important?
<--- Score

34. When are meeting minutes sent out? Who is on the distribution list?
<--- Score

35. How have you defined all Data communication requirements first?
<--- Score

36. What is out-of-scope initially?
<--- Score

37. Why are you doing Data communication and what is the scope?
<--- Score

38. Who are the Data communication improvement team members, including Management Leads and Coaches?
<--- Score

39. How often are the team meetings?
<--- Score

40. Do the problem and goal statements meet the SMART criteria (specific, measurable, attainable, relevant, and time-bound)?
<--- Score

41. Are different versions of process maps needed to account for the different types of inputs?
<--- Score

42. Is the work to date meeting requirements?
<--- Score

43. How will the Data communication team and the group measure complete success of Data communication?
<--- Score

44. What is the definition of Data communication excellence?
<--- Score

45. Is Data communication currently on schedule according to the plan?
<--- Score

46. The political context: who holds power?
<--- Score

47. What are the tasks and definitions?
<--- Score

48. What constraints exist that might impact the team?
<--- Score

49. Are the Data communication requirements complete?
<--- Score

50. Has the improvement team collected the 'voice of the customer' (obtained feedback – qualitative and quantitative)?
<--- Score

51. Has the Data communication work been fairly and/or equitably divided and delegated among team members who are qualified and capable to perform the work? Has everyone contributed?
<--- Score

52. Has/have the customer(s) been identified?
<--- Score

53. Has everyone on the team, including the team leaders, been properly trained?
<--- Score

54. Has a high-level 'as is' process map been completed, verified and validated?
<--- Score

55. Who defines (or who defined) the rules and roles?
<--- Score

56. Is the Data communication scope complete and appropriately sized?
<--- Score

57. Is the Data communication scope manageable?
<--- Score

58. Where can you gather more information?
<--- Score

59. Are approval levels defined for contracts and supplements to contracts?
<--- Score

60. What baselines are required to be defined and managed?
<--- Score

61. Is scope creep really all bad news?
<--- Score

62. Are accountability and ownership for Data communication clearly defined?
<--- Score

63. What are the rough order estimates on cost savings/opportunities that Data communication brings?
<--- Score

64. Is it clearly defined in and to your organization what you do?
<--- Score

65. When is the estimated completion date?
<--- Score

66. How can the value of Data communication be defined?
<--- Score

67. Is the scope of Data communication defined?
<--- Score

68. What are the Data communication use cases?
<--- Score

69. Is the improvement team aware of the different versions of a process: what they think it is vs. what it actually is vs. what it should be vs. what it could be?
<--- Score

70. Are there any constraints known that bear on the ability to perform Data communication work? How is the team addressing them?
<--- Score

71. In what way can you redefine the criteria of choice clients have in your category in your favor?
<--- Score

72. Is the team adequately staffed with the desired cross-functionality? If not, what additional resources are available to the team?
<--- Score

73. What Data communication services do you require?
<--- Score

74. Is the current 'as is' process being followed? If not, what are the discrepancies?
<--- Score

75. Are resources adequate for the scope?
<--- Score

76. Are all requirements met?
<--- Score

77. What are the boundaries of the scope? What is in bounds and what is not? What is the start point? What is the stop point?
<--- Score

78. How do you keep key subject matter experts in the loop?
<--- Score

79. How do you catch Data communication definition inconsistencies?
<--- Score

80. What sources do you use to gather information for a Data communication study?
<--- Score

81. What information should you gather?
<--- Score

82. Is there a completed, verified, and validated high-level 'as is' (not 'should be' or 'could be') stakeholder process map?
<--- Score

83. How will variation in the actual durations of each activity be dealt with to ensure that the expected Data communication results are met?
<--- Score

84. What gets examined?
<--- Score

85. What customer feedback methods were used to solicit their input?

<--- Score

86. Has the direction changed at all during the course of Data communication? If so, when did it change and why?
<--- Score

87. Is Data communication linked to key stakeholder goals and objectives?
<--- Score

88. Have all of the relationships been defined properly?
<--- Score

89. Who is gathering information?
<--- Score

90. What is in scope?
<--- Score

91. How did the Data communication manager receive input to the development of a Data communication improvement plan and the estimated completion dates/times of each activity?
<--- Score

92. What sort of initial information to gather?
<--- Score

93. How does the Data communication manager ensure against scope creep?
<--- Score

94. Is there any additional Data communication definition of success?

<--- Score

95. Are audit criteria, scope, frequency and methods defined?
<--- Score

96. What are the Roles and Responsibilities for each team member and its leadership? Where is this documented?
<--- Score

97. Scope of sensitive information?
<--- Score

98. What was the context?
<--- Score

99. What is the definition of success?
<--- Score

100. Has anyone else (internal or external to the group) attempted to solve this problem or a similar one before? If so, what knowledge can be leveraged from these previous efforts?
<--- Score

101. What information do you gather?
<--- Score

102. Has a Data communication requirement not been met?
<--- Score

103. What scope to assess?
<--- Score

104. How would you define Data communication leadership?
<--- Score

105. What are the requirements for audit information?
<--- Score

106. What key stakeholder process output measure(s) does Data communication leverage and how?
<--- Score

107. Have all basic functions of Data communication been defined?
<--- Score

108. What intelligence can you gather?
<--- Score

109. What defines best in class?
<--- Score

110. When is/was the Data communication start date?
<--- Score

111. How do you manage scope?
<--- Score

112. How is the team tracking and documenting its work?
<--- Score

113. What system do you use for gathering Data communication information?
<--- Score

114. Does the scope remain the same?

<--- Score

115. What is out of scope?
<--- Score

116. How do you gather the stories?
<--- Score

117. What would be the goal or target for a Data communication's improvement team?
<--- Score

118. Do you have organizational privacy requirements?
<--- Score

119. Who approved the Data communication scope?
<--- Score

120. Are there different segments of customers?
<--- Score

121. Is special Data communication user knowledge required?
<--- Score

122. Has a team charter been developed and communicated?
<--- Score

123. Have the customer needs been translated into specific, measurable requirements? How?
<--- Score

124. How do you gather requirements?
<--- Score

125. How do you build the right business case?
<--- Score

126. What is the scope of Data communication?
<--- Score

127. Does the team have regular meetings?
<--- Score

128. Do you all define Data communication in the same way?
<--- Score

129. Is there regularly 100% attendance at the team meetings? If not, have appointed substitutes attended to preserve cross-functionality and full representation?
<--- Score

130. Is the team equipped with available and reliable resources?
<--- Score

131. How do you manage unclear Data communication requirements?
<--- Score

132. Are roles and responsibilities formally defined?
<--- Score

Add up total points for this section:
_____ = Total points for this section

Divided by: ______ (number of statements answered) = ______

Average score for this section

Transfer your score to the Data communication Index at the beginning of the Self-Assessment.

# CRITERION #3: MEASURE:

INTENT: Gather the correct data. Measure the current performance and evolution of the situation.

In my belief, the answer to this question is clearly defined:

5 Strongly Agree

4 Agree

3 Neutral

2 Disagree

1 Strongly Disagree

1. What are your primary costs, revenues, assets?
<--- Score

2. What are the operational costs after Data communication deployment?
<--- Score

3. How is the value delivered by Data communication being measured?

<--- Score

4. Why a Data communication focus?
<--- Score

5. Where can you go to verify the info?
<--- Score

6. Are Data communication vulnerabilities categorized and prioritized?
<--- Score

7. Are missed Data communication opportunities costing your organization money?
<--- Score

8. Have you made assumptions about the shape of the future, particularly its impact on your customers and competitors?
<--- Score

9. Are indirect costs charged to the Data communication program?
<--- Score

10. Are the measurements objective?
<--- Score

11. What drives O&M cost?
<--- Score

12. How do you verify performance?
<--- Score

13. Are the units of measure consistent?
<--- Score

14. What causes innovation to fail or succeed in your organization?
<--- Score

15. What is your Data communication quality cost segregation study?
<--- Score

16. How will your organization measure success?
<--- Score

17. Will Data communication have an impact on current business continuity, disaster recovery processes and/or infrastructure?
<--- Score

18. Have you included everything in your Data communication cost models?
<--- Score

19. What would be a real cause for concern?
<--- Score

20. How do you measure efficient delivery of Data communication services?
<--- Score

21. What causes investor action?
<--- Score

22. How much does it cost?
<--- Score

23. What does your operating model cost?
<--- Score

24. What are the uncertainties surrounding estimates of impact?
<--- Score

25. How do you verify the authenticity of the data and information used?
<--- Score

26. How are costs allocated?
<--- Score

27. Why do you expend time and effort to implement measurement, for whom?
<--- Score

28. Why do the measurements/indicators matter?
<--- Score

29. How long to keep data and how to manage retention costs?
<--- Score

30. Is the cost worth the Data communication effort ?
<--- Score

**31. What is the cost of data communication from deployment sites to backend systems?**
<--- Score

32. How will you measure your Data communication effectiveness?
<--- Score

33. When a disaster occurs, who gets priority?
<--- Score

34. What are your customers expectations and measures?
<--- Score

35. Do you have an issue in getting priority?
<--- Score

36. How can a Data communication test verify your ideas or assumptions?
<--- Score

37. How do you measure variability?
<--- Score

38. How do your measurements capture actionable Data communication information for use in exceeding your customers expectations and securing your customers engagement?
<--- Score

39. Are there measurements based on task performance?
<--- Score

40. Who is involved in verifying compliance?
<--- Score

41. Do you aggressively reward and promote the people who have the biggest impact on creating excellent Data communication services/products?
<--- Score

42. What causes extra work or rework?
<--- Score

43. How sensitive must the Data communication strategy be to cost?
<--- Score

44. Are there competing Data communication priorities?
<--- Score

45. When are costs are incurred?
<--- Score

46. What is the total fixed cost?
<--- Score

47. Which Data communication impacts are significant?
<--- Score

48. Are you taking your company in the direction of better and revenue or cheaper and cost?
<--- Score

49. How can you reduce costs?
<--- Score

50. How can you reduce the costs of obtaining inputs?
<--- Score

51. How do you verify if Data communication is built right?
<--- Score

52. Do you effectively measure and reward individual and team performance?
<--- Score

53. How will measures be used to manage and adapt?
<--- Score

54. Are you aware of what could cause a problem?
<--- Score

55. Are actual costs in line with budgeted costs?
<--- Score

56. How will success or failure be measured?
<--- Score

57. The approach of traditional Data communication works for detail complexity but is focused on a systematic approach rather than an understanding of the nature of systems themselves, what approach will permit your organization to deal with the kind of unpredictable emergent behaviors that dynamic complexity can introduce?
<--- Score

58. Does the Data communication task fit the client's priorities?
<--- Score

59. What are the current costs of the Data communication process?
<--- Score

60. How can you manage cost down?
<--- Score

61. What tests verify requirements?
<--- Score

62. How frequently do you track Data communication

measures?
<--- Score

63. What could cause delays in the schedule?
<--- Score

64. How do you verify the Data communication requirements quality?
<--- Score

65. Have design-to-cost goals been established?
<--- Score

66. Is there an opportunity to verify requirements?
<--- Score

67. Where is it measured?
<--- Score

68. What could cause you to change course?
<--- Score

69. Among the Data communication product and service cost to be estimated, which is considered hardest to estimate?
<--- Score

70. What are the costs and benefits?
<--- Score

71. What is your decision requirements diagram?
<--- Score

72. What is the cause of any Data communication gaps?
<--- Score

73. Are you able to realize any cost savings?
<--- Score

74. Are there any easy-to-implement alternatives to Data communication? Sometimes other solutions are available that do not require the cost implications of a full-blown project?
<--- Score

75. How can you measure the performance?
<--- Score

**76. Do you provide overall system and/or application architecture diagrams including a full description of the data communications architecture for all components of the system?**
<--- Score

77. How can you measure Data communication in a systematic way?
<--- Score

78. What are your operating costs?
<--- Score

79. What are the costs of delaying Data communication action?
<--- Score

80. What are hidden Data communication quality costs?
<--- Score

81. What would it cost to replace your technology?
<--- Score

82. How do you quantify and qualify impacts?
<--- Score

83. What users will be impacted?
<--- Score

84. How do you verify and validate the Data communication data?
<--- Score

85. Is the solution cost-effective?
<--- Score

86. Has a cost center been established?
<--- Score

87. What can be used to verify compliance?
<--- Score

88. What measurements are possible, practicable and meaningful?
<--- Score

89. What measurements are being captured?
<--- Score

90. How do you prevent mis-estimating cost?
<--- Score

91. Does management have the right priorities among projects?
<--- Score

92. Do you verify that corrective actions were taken?
<--- Score

93. How will effects be measured?
<--- Score

94. What is the Data communication business impact?
<--- Score

95. Which costs should be taken into account?
<--- Score

96. How do you measure lifecycle phases?
<--- Score

97. Are supply costs steady or fluctuating?
<--- Score

98. What are allowable costs?
<--- Score

99. Was a business case (cost/benefit) developed?
<--- Score

100. What does a Test Case verify?
<--- Score

101. Who pays the cost?
<--- Score

102. What are you verifying?
<--- Score

103. What does verifying compliance entail?
<--- Score

104. What are your key Data communication organizational performance measures, including key

short and longer-term financial measures?
<--- Score

105. How are measurements made?
<--- Score

106. How will you measure success?
<--- Score

107. Who should receive measurement reports?
<--- Score

108. When should you bother with diagrams?
<--- Score

109. How do you measure success?
<--- Score

110. What causes mismanagement?
<--- Score

111. What is the total cost related to deploying Data communication, including any consulting or professional services?
<--- Score

112. What relevant entities could be measured?
<--- Score

113. What potential environmental factors impact the Data communication effort?
<--- Score

114. What do you measure and why?
<--- Score

115. What are the costs of reform?
<--- Score

116. What disadvantage does this cause for the user?
<--- Score

117. How are you verifying it?
<--- Score

118. What harm might be caused?
<--- Score

119. What does losing customers cost your organization?
<--- Score

120. Did you tackle the cause or the symptom?
<--- Score

121. What is an unallowable cost?
<--- Score

122. What are the Data communication key cost drivers?
<--- Score

123. Is it possible to estimate the impact of unanticipated complexity such as wrong or failed assumptions, feedback, etcetera on proposed reforms?
<--- Score

124. What are the costs?
<--- Score

125. How will costs be allocated?

<--- Score

126. How is progress measured?
<--- Score

127. Does a Data communication quantification method exist?
<--- Score

128. Which measures and indicators matter?
<--- Score

129. How do you verify your resources?
<--- Score

130. What are the strategic priorities for this year?
<--- Score

131. What are the Data communication investment costs?
<--- Score

132. What happens if cost savings do not materialize?
<--- Score

Add up total points for this section:
_____ = Total points for this section

Divided by: ______ (number of statements answered) = ______
Average score for this section

Transfer your score to the Data communication Index at the beginning of the Self-Assessment.

# CRITERION #4: ANALYZE:

INTENT: Analyze causes, assumptions and hypotheses.

In my belief, the answer to this question is clearly defined:

5 Strongly Agree

4 Agree

3 Neutral

2 Disagree

1 Strongly Disagree

1. How difficult is it to qualify what Data communication ROI is?
<--- Score

2. What qualifications and skills do you need?
<--- Score

3. Have you defined which data is gathered how?
<--- Score

4. What do you need to qualify?
<--- Score

5. Who qualifies to gain access to data?
<--- Score

6. How are outputs preserved and protected?
<--- Score

**7. Are specialized data communications needed?**
<--- Score

8. Are Data communication changes recognized early enough to be approved through the regular process?
<--- Score

9. What systems/processes must you excel at?
<--- Score

10. Who will gather what data?
<--- Score

11. A compounding model resolution with available relevant data can often provide insight towards a solution methodology; which Data communication models, tools and techniques are necessary?
<--- Score

**12. Does your system seamlessly allow for both voice and data communications?**
<--- Score

13. Where is Data communication data gathered?
<--- Score

14. What are the personnel training and qualifications

required?
<--- Score

15. What are the necessary qualifications?
<--- Score

16. What qualifications are needed?
<--- Score

17. What are your current levels and trends in key Data communication measures or indicators of product and process performance that are important to and directly serve your customers?
<--- Score

18. What resources go in to get the desired output?
<--- Score

**19. What is the purpose of the network layer in data communications?**
<--- Score

20. Who owns what data?
<--- Score

21. What data is gathered?
<--- Score

22. What information qualified as important?
<--- Score

23. What are the best opportunities for value improvement?
<--- Score

**24. Who needs the ability for data communications**

**from fixed points?**
<--- Score

25. How do you ensure that the Data communication opportunity is realistic?
<--- Score

26. What is your organizations system for selecting qualified vendors?
<--- Score

27. How can risk management be tied procedurally to process elements?
<--- Score

28. Should you invest in industry-recognized qualifications?
<--- Score

29. Record-keeping requirements flow from the records needed as inputs, outputs, controls and for transformation of a Data communication process, are the records needed as inputs to the Data communication process available?
<--- Score

30. What other jobs or tasks affect the performance of the steps in the Data communication process?
<--- Score

31. What were the crucial 'moments of truth' on the process map?
<--- Score

32. How is the way you as the leader think and process information affecting your organizational culture?

<--- Score

33. Do you have the authority to produce the output?
<--- Score

34. When should a process be art not science?
<--- Score

35. What will drive Data communication change?
<--- Score

36. Do your employees have the opportunity to do what they do best everyday?
<--- Score

37. What internal processes need improvement?
<--- Score

38. How is data used for program management and improvement?
<--- Score

39. What is your organizations process which leads to recognition of value generation?
<--- Score

40. Has an output goal been set?
<--- Score

41. What are evaluation criteria for the output?
<--- Score

**42. What do you want your organizations future system for voice and data communications to look like?**
<--- Score

43. What process should you select for improvement?
<--- Score

44. What methods do you use to gather Data communication data?
<--- Score

45. How is the data gathered?
<--- Score

46. Do quality systems drive continuous improvement?
<--- Score

47. Who gets your output?
<--- Score

**48. Will there be new data communication (data drop) locations?**
<--- Score

**49. High-throughput satellites are able to bring large amounts of capacity to be used for data communications, and who will consume this capacity?**
<--- Score

50. What tools were used to narrow the list of possible causes?
<--- Score

**51. Why does the systems designer need to have some knowledge of data communications?**
<--- Score

52. How do you define collaboration and team output?
<--- Score

53. What qualifications do Data communication leaders need?
<--- Score

**54. How should a complete, coherent data communications security solution be defined?**
<--- Score

**55. How to integrate the information globally by making the data communication capability of computers?**
<--- Score

56. What are your current levels and trends in key measures or indicators of Data communication product and process performance that are important to and directly serve your customers? How do these results compare with the performance of your competitors and other organizations with similar offerings?
<--- Score

57. What are your key performance measures or indicators and in-process measures for the control and improvement of your Data communication processes?
<--- Score

**58. What is your data communication status?**
<--- Score

59. Is the final output clearly identified?

<--- Score

60. What, related to, Data communication processes does your organization outsource?
<--- Score

**61. Do you run a data communications network?**
<--- Score

**62. Why optical data communications and why now?**
<--- Score

**63. Where will the help desks or command centers be located and are there resources available to accommodate additional voice and data communication?**
<--- Score

64. What are the processes for audit reporting and management?
<--- Score

65. Are all staff in core Data communication subjects Highly Qualified?
<--- Score

66. What Data communication metrics are outputs of the process?
<--- Score

67. Is there a strict change management process?
<--- Score

68. Do staff qualifications match your project?
<--- Score

**69. How great is the need for mobile data communications in your jurisdiction?**
<--- Score

70. Which Data communication data should be retained?
<--- Score

71. What tools were used to generate the list of possible causes?
<--- Score

72. What qualifications are necessary?
<--- Score

73. What controls do you have in place to protect data?
<--- Score

74. Is there any way to speed up the process?
<--- Score

75. How often will data be collected for measures?
<--- Score

76. What kind of crime could a potential new hire have committed that would not only not disqualify him/her from being hired by your organization, but would actually indicate that he/she might be a particularly good fit?
<--- Score

77. What Data communication data will be collected?
<--- Score

78. How is the Data communication Value Stream Mapping managed?
<--- Score

79. Do you, as a leader, bounce back quickly from setbacks?
<--- Score

80. How do you identify specific Data communication investment opportunities and emerging trends?
<--- Score

81. What other organizational variables, such as reward systems or communication systems, affect the performance of this Data communication process?
<--- Score

82. What are the Data communication design outputs?
<--- Score

83. What quality tools were used to get through the analyze phase?
<--- Score

84. Can you add value to the current Data communication decision-making process (largely qualitative) by incorporating uncertainty modeling (more quantitative)?
<--- Score

85. Do your contracts/agreements contain data security obligations?
<--- Score

**86. Are specialized data communications required**

**to transfer information to or from the application?**
<--- Score

87. Who is involved in the management review process?
<--- Score

88. What are your Data communication processes?
<--- Score

**89. How quickly could data communications facilities be restored?**
<--- Score

90. How will the Data communication data be captured?
<--- Score

91. Think about some of the processes you undertake within your organization, which do you own?
<--- Score

92. Are you missing Data communication opportunities?
<--- Score

93. Do you understand your management processes today?
<--- Score

94. How will the change process be managed?
<--- Score

95. Is pre-qualification of suppliers carried out?
<--- Score

96. How has the Data communication data been gathered?
<--- Score

97. What are the Data communication business drivers?
<--- Score

98. What types of data do your Data communication indicators require?
<--- Score

99. What qualifies as competition?
<--- Score

100. How do you implement and manage your work processes to ensure that they meet design requirements?
<--- Score

101. Where can you get qualified talent today?
<--- Score

102. What successful thing are you doing today that may be blinding you to new growth opportunities?
<--- Score

**103. Are there recovery procedures for a failure of data communications equipment or software?**
<--- Score

104. How is Data communication data gathered?
<--- Score

105. Are your outputs consistent?
<--- Score

106. What are your best practices for minimizing Data communication project risk, while demonstrating incremental value and quick wins throughout the Data communication project lifecycle?
<--- Score

107. An organizationally feasible system request is one that considers the mission, goals and objectives of the organization, key questions are: is the Data communication solution request practical and will it solve a problem or take advantage of an opportunity to achieve company goals?
<--- Score

108. How do you promote understanding that opportunity for improvement is not criticism of the status quo, or the people who created the status quo?
<--- Score

109. What is the Value Stream Mapping?
<--- Score

110. Identify an operational issue in your organization, for example, could a particular task be done more quickly or more efficiently by Data communication?
<--- Score

111. Who will facilitate the team and process?
<--- Score

**112. Are data communications required?**
<--- Score

**113. How does cellular circuit data work?**
<--- Score

114. What is the oversight process?
<--- Score

115. What Data communication data do you gather or use now?
<--- Score

116. How do you measure the operational performance of your key work systems and processes, including productivity, cycle time, and other appropriate measures of process effectiveness, efficiency, and innovation?
<--- Score

**117. What corporate structures and governance drive performance for resilience?**
<--- Score

118. Who is involved with workflow mapping?
<--- Score

**119. How do you ensure the privacy of data communications?**
<--- Score

**120. What are the different kinds of wireless data communication technologies used?**
<--- Score

121. Is the suppliers process defined and controlled?
<--- Score

**122. How can you ensure the privacy of data communications?**
<--- Score

123. What are the disruptive Data communication technologies that enable your organization to radically change your business processes?
<--- Score

**124. How will you enforce scalable and secure data communications with multiple isolated IoT vendors?**
<--- Score

**125. What data communication aspects does the specification address?**
<--- Score

126. Do your leaders quickly bounce back from setbacks?
<--- Score

127. How will the data be checked for quality?
<--- Score

128. What were the financial benefits resulting from any 'ground fruit or low-hanging fruit' (quick fixes)?
<--- Score

129. What is the Data communication Driver?
<--- Score

**130. What are data communications links?**
<--- Score

131. What process improvements will be needed?
<--- Score

132. How do you use Data communication data

and information to support organizational decision making and innovation?
<--- Score

**133. Does your organization have data communication networks?**
<--- Score

134. How much data can be collected in the given timeframe?
<--- Score

**135. What type of agreements are in place with data communications suppliers?**
<--- Score

**136. By what means do the main telephone and data communications interface it or building?**
<--- Score

137. How will corresponding data be collected?
<--- Score

138. What Data communication data should be managed?
<--- Score

139. Is there an established change management process?
<--- Score

140. Are all team members qualified for all tasks?
<--- Score

141. How does the organization define, manage, and improve its Data communication processes?

<--- Score

**142. What are the main reasons behind the need of data communication?**

<--- Score

Add up total points for this section:
_____ = Total points for this section

Divided by: ______ (number of statements answered) = ______
Average score for this section

Transfer your score to the Data communication Index at the beginning of the Self-Assessment.

# CRITERION #5: IMPROVE:

INTENT: Develop a practical solution. Innovate, establish and test the solution and to measure the results.

In my belief, the answer to this question is clearly defined:

5 Strongly Agree

4 Agree

3 Neutral

2 Disagree

1 Strongly Disagree

1. Do vendor agreements bring new compliance risk ?
<--- Score

2. Who will be using the results of the measurement activities?
<--- Score

3. What are the concrete Data communication results?
<--- Score

4. Who makes the Data communication decisions in your organization?
<--- Score

5. Do you cover the five essential competencies: Communication, Collaboration,Innovation, Adaptability, and Leadership that improve an organizations ability to leverage the new Data communication in a volatile global economy?
<--- Score

6. Who will be responsible for documenting the Data communication requirements in detail?
<--- Score

7. What tools were used to tap into the creativity and encourage 'outside the box' thinking?
<--- Score

8. Who are the Data communication decision-makers?
<--- Score

9. Where do the Data communication decisions reside?
<--- Score

10. Risk Identification: What are the possible risk events your organization faces in relation to Data communication?
<--- Score

11. What are your current levels and trends in key measures or indicators of workforce and leader development?
<--- Score

12. Have you identified breakpoints and/or risk tolerances that will trigger broad consideration of a potential need for intervention or modification of strategy?
<--- Score

13. For decision problems, how do you develop a decision statement?
<--- Score

14. Can you identify any significant risks or exposures to Data communication third- parties (vendors, service providers, alliance partners etc) that concern you?
<--- Score

15. In the past few months, what is the smallest change you have made that has had the biggest positive result? What was it about that small change that produced the large return?
<--- Score

16. Are events managed to resolution?
<--- Score

17. How do you measure risk?
<--- Score

18. What alternative responses are available to manage risk?
<--- Score

19. How can you improve performance?
<--- Score

20. What resources are required for the improvement efforts?
<--- Score

21. How can skill-level changes improve Data communication?
<--- Score

22. What needs improvement? Why?
<--- Score

23. Is risk periodically assessed?
<--- Score

24. Do you need to do a usability evaluation?
<--- Score

25. How do you measure improved Data communication service perception, and satisfaction?
<--- Score

26. What improvements have been achieved?
<--- Score

27. How is continuous improvement applied to risk management?
<--- Score

28. Will the controls trigger any other risks?
<--- Score

29. How scalable is your Data communication solution?
<--- Score

30. What can you do to improve?

<--- Score

31. Who manages supplier risk management in your organization?
<--- Score

32. What tools were most useful during the improve phase?
<--- Score

33. Who controls key decisions that will be made?
<--- Score

34. How is knowledge sharing about risk management improved?
<--- Score

35. Is any Data communication documentation required?
<--- Score

36. Explorations of the frontiers of Data communication will help you build influence, improve Data communication, optimize decision making, and sustain change, what is your approach?
<--- Score

37. What practices helps your organization to develop its capacity to recognize patterns?
<--- Score

38. What is the team's contingency plan for potential problems occurring in implementation?
<--- Score

39. How do you go about comparing Data

communication approaches/solutions?
<--- Score

40. Are risk management tasks balanced centrally and locally?
<--- Score

41. What assumptions are made about the solution and approach?
<--- Score

42. Can you integrate quality management and risk management?
<--- Score

43. How will you measure the results?
<--- Score

44. Have you achieved Data communication improvements?
<--- Score

45. What were the underlying assumptions on the cost-benefit analysis?
<--- Score

46. Are the most efficient solutions problem-specific?
<--- Score

47. How will you know that a change is an improvement?
<--- Score

48. What are the affordable Data communication risks?
<--- Score

49. Was a Data communication charter developed?
<--- Score

50. Does the goal represent a desired result that can be measured?
<--- Score

51. How do you improve productivity?
<--- Score

52. For estimation problems, how do you develop an estimation statement?
<--- Score

53. What strategies for Data communication improvement are successful?
<--- Score

54. Is the Data communication documentation thorough?
<--- Score

55. Is the Data communication risk managed?
<--- Score

56. What Data communication improvements can be made?
<--- Score

57. What are the implications of the one critical Data communication decision 10 minutes, 10 months, and 10 years from now?
<--- Score

58. If you could go back in time five years, what

decision would you make differently? What is your best guess as to what decision you're making today you might regret five years from now?
<--- Score

59. Do you combine technical expertise with business knowledge and Data communication Key topics include lifecycles, development approaches, requirements and how to make a business case?
<--- Score

60. What lessons, if any, from a pilot were incorporated into the design of the full-scale solution?
<--- Score

61. How do you link measurement and risk?
<--- Score

62. To what extent does management recognize Data communication as a tool to increase the results?
<--- Score

63. Who are the Data communication decision makers?
<--- Score

64. What actually has to improve and by how much?
<--- Score

65. How risky is your organization?
<--- Score

66. Is Data communication documentation maintained?
<--- Score

67. Is there any other Data communication solution?
<--- Score

68. What should a proof of concept or pilot accomplish?
<--- Score

69. What were the criteria for evaluating a Data communication pilot?
<--- Score

70. What tools do you use once you have decided on a Data communication strategy and more importantly how do you choose?
<--- Score

71. How will you know that you have improved?
<--- Score

72. Risk events: what are the things that could go wrong?
<--- Score

73. How do you define the solutions' scope?
<--- Score

74. How do you mitigate Data communication risk?
<--- Score

75. Data communication risk decisions: whose call Is It?
<--- Score

76. What current systems have to be understood and/ or changed?
<--- Score

77. Are procedures documented for managing Data communication risks?
<--- Score

78. What risks do you need to manage?
<--- Score

79. Are the risks fully understood, reasonable and manageable?
<--- Score

80. Is supporting Data communication documentation required?
<--- Score

81. What is the risk?
<--- Score

82. How will you recognize and celebrate results?
<--- Score

83. What is the Data communication's sustainability risk?
<--- Score

84. What is Data communication risk?
<--- Score

85. Would you develop a Data communication Communication Strategy?
<--- Score

86. Does a good decision guarantee a good outcome?
<--- Score

87. What do you want to improve?
<--- Score

88. Are the key business and technology risks being managed?
<--- Score

89. What criteria will you use to assess your Data communication risks?
<--- Score

90. What are the expected Data communication results?
<--- Score

91. How are Data communication risks managed?
<--- Score

92. What is Data communication's impact on utilizing the best solution(s)?
<--- Score

93. What are the Data communication security risks?
<--- Score

94. Is the Data communication solution sustainable?
<--- Score

95. Are you assessing Data communication and risk?
<--- Score

96. How do the Data communication results compare with the performance of your competitors and other organizations with similar offerings?
<--- Score

97. How do you decide how much to remunerate an employee?
<--- Score

98. How significant is the improvement in the eyes of the end user?
<--- Score

99. How are policy decisions made and where?
<--- Score

100. How does your organization evaluate strategic Data communication success?
<--- Score

101. Do those selected for the Data communication team have a good general understanding of what Data communication is all about?
<--- Score

102. Who manages Data communication risk?
<--- Score

103. What to do with the results or outcomes of measurements?
<--- Score

104. How do you manage and improve your Data communication work systems to deliver customer value and achieve organizational success and sustainability?
<--- Score

105. How will you know when its improved?
<--- Score

106. Is there a high likelihood that any recommendations will achieve their intended results?
<--- Score

107. Do you have the optimal project management team structure?
<--- Score

108. How do you keep improving Data communication?
<--- Score

109. How do you improve Data communication service perception, and satisfaction?
<--- Score

110. Where do you need Data communication improvement?
<--- Score

111. Who do you report Data communication results to?
<--- Score

**112. How do other organizations integrate resilience into enterprise risk management structures?**
<--- Score

113. How do you manage Data communication risk?
<--- Score

114. Which Data communication solution is appropriate?
<--- Score

115. Who are the key stakeholders for the Data communication evaluation?
<--- Score

116. How do you deal with Data communication risk?
<--- Score

117. How can you improve Data communication?
<--- Score

118. What is the implementation plan?
<--- Score

119. Are risk triggers captured?
<--- Score

120. What tools were used to evaluate the potential solutions?
<--- Score

121. Is the measure of success for Data communication understandable to a variety of people?
<--- Score

122. Who controls the risk?
<--- Score

123. Which of the recognised risks out of all risks can be most likely transferred?
<--- Score

124. Is the solution technically practical?
<--- Score

125. Why improve in the first place?

<--- Score

126. At what point will vulnerability assessments be performed once Data communication is put into production (e.g., ongoing Risk Management after implementation)?
<--- Score

127. What error proofing will be done to address some of the discrepancies observed in the 'as is' process?
<--- Score

128. How can you better manage risk?
<--- Score

129. What is the magnitude of the improvements?
<--- Score

130. How do you measure progress and evaluate training effectiveness?
<--- Score

Add up total points for this section:
_____ = Total points for this section

Divided by: ______ (number of statements answered) = ______ Average score for this section

Transfer your score to the Data communication Index at the beginning of the Self-Assessment.

# CRITERION #6: CONTROL:

INTENT: Implement the practical solution. Maintain the performance and correct possible complications.

In my belief, the answer to this question is clearly defined:

5 Strongly Agree

4 Agree

3 Neutral

2 Disagree

1 Strongly Disagree

1. What key inputs and outputs are being measured on an ongoing basis?
<--- Score

2. What is the recommended frequency of auditing?
<--- Score

3. Will the team be available to assist members in planning investigations?

<--- Score

4. Do the viable solutions scale to future needs?
<--- Score

5. What is the standard for acceptable Data communication performance?
<--- Score

6. What is the control/monitoring plan?
<--- Score

7. Have new or revised work instructions resulted?
<--- Score

8. How do you select, collect, align, and integrate Data communication data and information for tracking daily operations and overall organizational performance, including progress relative to strategic objectives and action plans?
<--- Score

9. Are pertinent alerts monitored, analyzed and distributed to appropriate personnel?
<--- Score

10. Does a troubleshooting guide exist or is it needed?
<--- Score

11. What are the known security controls?
<--- Score

12. How will the process owner and team be able to hold the gains?
<--- Score

13. Are documented procedures clear and easy to follow for the operators?
<--- Score

14. Is there a recommended audit plan for routine surveillance inspections of Data communication's gains?
<--- Score

15. How might the group capture best practices and lessons learned so as to leverage improvements?
<--- Score

16. What adjustments to the strategies are needed?
<--- Score

17. In the case of a Data communication project, the criteria for the audit derive from implementation objectives, an audit of a Data communication project involves assessing whether the recommendations outlined for implementation have been met, can you track that any Data communication project is implemented as planned, and is it working?
<--- Score

18. What other areas of the group might benefit from the Data communication team's improvements, knowledge, and learning?
<--- Score

19. What quality tools were useful in the control phase?
<--- Score

20. What are the key elements of your Data communication performance improvement system,

including your evaluation, organizational learning, and innovation processes?
<--- Score

21. What is your plan to assess your security risks?
<--- Score

22. Who is the Data communication process owner?
<--- Score

23. Has the improved process and its steps been standardized?
<--- Score

24. Is there a standardized process?
<--- Score

25. Are you measuring, monitoring and predicting Data communication activities to optimize operations and profitability, and enhancing outcomes?
<--- Score

26. What Data communication standards are applicable?
<--- Score

27. How do your controls stack up?
<--- Score

28. How do you spread information?
<--- Score

29. Is the Data communication test/monitoring cost justified?
<--- Score

30. How will the process owner verify improvement in present and future sigma levels, process capabilities?
<--- Score

31. What do you measure to verify effectiveness gains?
<--- Score

32. Is new knowledge gained imbedded in the response plan?
<--- Score

33. Who sets the Data communication standards?
<--- Score

34. Is there a documented and implemented monitoring plan?
<--- Score

35. What is the best design framework for Data communication organization now that, in a post industrial-age if the top-down, command and control model is no longer relevant?
<--- Score

36. Are there documented procedures?
<--- Score

37. Are suggested corrective/restorative actions indicated on the response plan for known causes to problems that might surface?
<--- Score

38. How do senior leaders actions reflect a commitment to the organizations Data communication values?

<--- Score

39. Does the response plan contain a definite closed loop continual improvement scheme (e.g., plan-do-check-act)?
<--- Score

40. Do the Data communication decisions you make today help people and the planet tomorrow?
<--- Score

41. Will any special training be provided for results interpretation?
<--- Score

42. How widespread is its use?
<--- Score

43. How do you plan on providing proper recognition and disclosure of supporting companies?
<--- Score

44. Is there documentation that will support the successful operation of the improvement?
<--- Score

45. How will the day-to-day responsibilities for monitoring and continual improvement be transferred from the improvement team to the process owner?
<--- Score

46. Who is going to spread your message?
<--- Score

47. Are the planned controls in place?

<--- Score

48. Who will be in control?
<--- Score

49. Are operating procedures consistent?
<--- Score

50. What are you attempting to measure/monitor?
<--- Score

51. Are new process steps, standards, and documentation ingrained into normal operations?
<--- Score

52. Is knowledge gained on process shared and institutionalized?
<--- Score

53. Does the Data communication performance meet the customer's requirements?
<--- Score

54. What are customers monitoring?
<--- Score

55. Can support from partners be adjusted?
<--- Score

56. What are the critical parameters to watch?
<--- Score

57. What do your reports reflect?
<--- Score

58. What should the next improvement project be

that is related to Data communication?
<--- Score

59. Are the planned controls working?
<--- Score

60. Will existing staff require re-training, for example, to learn new business processes?
<--- Score

61. Against what alternative is success being measured?
<--- Score

62. Is a response plan in place for when the input, process, or output measures indicate an 'out-of-control' condition?
<--- Score

63. How will input, process, and output variables be checked to detect for sub-optimal conditions?
<--- Score

64. What should you measure to verify efficiency gains?
<--- Score

65. Does Data communication appropriately measure and monitor risk?
<--- Score

66. Does job training on the documented procedures need to be part of the process team's education and training?
<--- Score

67. What is your theory of human motivation, and how does your compensation plan fit with that view?
<--- Score

68. Is reporting being used or needed?
<--- Score

69. Will your goals reflect your program budget?
<--- Score

70. Are controls in place and consistently applied?
<--- Score

71. Has the Data communication value of standards been quantified?
<--- Score

72. What are your results for key measures or indicators of the accomplishment of your Data communication strategy and action plans, including building and strengthening core competencies?
<--- Score

73. Is a response plan established and deployed?
<--- Score

74. Is there a transfer of ownership and knowledge to process owner and process team tasked with the responsibilities.
<--- Score

75. How will you measure your QA plan's effectiveness?
<--- Score

76. How will report readings be checked to effectively

monitor performance?
<--- Score

77. Can you adapt and adjust to changing Data communication situations?
<--- Score

78. Who has control over resources?
<--- Score

79. What can you control?
<--- Score

80. What are the performance and scale of the Data communication tools?
<--- Score

81. How will new or emerging customer needs/ requirements be checked/communicated to orient the process toward meeting the new specifications and continually reducing variation?
<--- Score

82. How is Data communication project cost planned, managed, monitored?
<--- Score

83. Is there a control plan in place for sustaining improvements (short and long-term)?
<--- Score

84. Do you monitor the Data communication decisions made and fine tune them as they evolve?
<--- Score

85. Implementation Planning: is a pilot needed to test

the changes before a full roll out occurs?
<--- Score

86. What other systems, operations, processes, and infrastructures (hiring practices, staffing, training, incentives/rewards, metrics/dashboards/scorecards, etc.) need updates, additions, changes, or deletions in order to facilitate knowledge transfer and improvements?
<--- Score

87. How do controls support value?
<--- Score

88. Where do ideas that reach policy makers and planners as proposals for Data communication strengthening and reform actually originate?
<--- Score

89. How likely is the current Data communication plan to come in on schedule or on budget?
<--- Score

Add up total points for this section:
_____ = Total points for this section

Divided by: ______ (number of statements answered) = ______ Average score for this section

Transfer your score to the Data communication Index at the beginning of the Self-Assessment.

# CRITERION #7: SUSTAIN:

INTENT: Retain the benefits.

In my belief, the answer to this question is clearly defined:

5 Strongly Agree

4 Agree

3 Neutral

2 Disagree

1 Strongly Disagree

1. Has implementation been effective in reaching specified objectives so far?
<--- Score

2. What is your question? Why?
<--- Score

3. What unique value proposition (UVP) do you offer?
<--- Score

4. What are current Data communication paradigms?

<--- Score

5. Who is responsible for errors?
<--- Score

6. Where can you break convention?
<--- Score

7. Are your responses positive or negative?
<--- Score

8. What is the range of capabilities?
<--- Score

9. Is there a work around that you can use?
<--- Score

10. What must you excel at?
<--- Score

11. In retrospect, of the projects that you pulled the plug on, what percent do you wish had been allowed to keep going, and what percent do you wish had ended earlier?
<--- Score

12. What are the usability implications of Data communication actions?
<--- Score

13. What is effective Data communication?
<--- Score

14. How do you deal with Data communication changes?
<--- Score

15. Is the Data communication organization completing tasks effectively and efficiently?
<--- Score

16. What is the estimated value of the project?
<--- Score

17. How can you become the company that would put you out of business?
<--- Score

18. What is the source of the strategies for Data communication strengthening and reform?
<--- Score

19. What happens at your organization when people fail?
<--- Score

20. How do you listen to customers to obtain actionable information?
<--- Score

21. Why should people listen to you?
<--- Score

22. What was the last experiment you ran?
<--- Score

23. How important is Data communication to the user organizations mission?
<--- Score

24. What projects are going on in the organization today, and what resources are those projects using

from the resource pools?
<--- Score

25. Think of your Data communication project, what are the main functions?
<--- Score

26. Do you think Data communication accomplishes the goals you expect it to accomplish?
<--- Score

27. Which models, tools and techniques are necessary?
<--- Score

28. Marketing budgets are tighter, consumers are more skeptical, and social media has changed forever the way we talk about Data communication, how do you gain traction?
<--- Score

29. How likely is it that a customer would recommend your company to a friend or colleague?
<--- Score

**30. How do you give a more complete, comprehensive situational awareness view to a soldier?**
<--- Score

31. How do you track customer value, profitability or financial return, organizational success, and sustainability?
<--- Score

32. How do you assess the Data communication

pitfalls that are inherent in implementing it?
<--- Score

33. If no one would ever find out about your accomplishments, how would you lead differently?
<--- Score

34. In a project to restructure Data communication outcomes, which stakeholders would you involve?
<--- Score

35. What are internal and external Data communication relations?
<--- Score

36. What information is critical to your organization that your executives are ignoring?
<--- Score

37. What is your formula for success in Data communication ?
<--- Score

38. What you are going to do to affect the numbers?
<--- Score

39. What one word do you want to own in the minds of your customers, employees, and partners?
<--- Score

40. Who is responsible for ensuring appropriate resources (time, people and money) are allocated to Data communication?
<--- Score

41. What are the barriers to increased Data

communication production?
<--- Score

42. How do you transition from the baseline to the target?
<--- Score

43. What is your BATNA (best alternative to a negotiated agreement)?
<--- Score

44. What business benefits will Data communication goals deliver if achieved?
<--- Score

45. Who else should you help?
<--- Score

46. How can you negotiate Data communication successfully with a stubborn boss, an irate client, or a deceitful coworker?
<--- Score

47. How do you manage Data communication Knowledge Management (KM)?
<--- Score

48. Who do you want your customers to become?
<--- Score

49. Are the criteria for selecting recommendations stated?
<--- Score

50. How do senior leaders deploy your organizations vision and values through your leadership system, to

the workforce, to key suppliers and partners, and to customers and other stakeholders, as appropriate?
<--- Score

51. Do you know what you are doing? And who do you call if you don't?
<--- Score

52. Do you have the right people on the bus?
<--- Score

53. How does Data communication integrate with other stakeholder initiatives?
<--- Score

54. What is the craziest thing you can do?
<--- Score

55. If your customer were your grandmother, would you tell her to buy what you're selling?
<--- Score

56. How can you become more high-tech but still be high touch?
<--- Score

57. What is the recommended frequency of auditing?
<--- Score

58. Do you think you know, or do you know you know ?
<--- Score

59. How do you create buy-in?
<--- Score

60. How can you incorporate support to ensure safe and effective use of Data communication into the services that you provide?
<--- Score

61. What could happen if you do not do it?
<--- Score

62. Can you maintain your growth without detracting from the factors that have contributed to your success?
<--- Score

63. What are the top 3 things at the forefront of your Data communication agendas for the next 3 years?
<--- Score

64. What potential megatrends could make your business model obsolete?
<--- Score

65. Are you / should you be revolutionary or evolutionary?
<--- Score

66. What relationships among Data communication trends do you perceive?
<--- Score

67. How do you engage the workforce, in addition to satisfying them?
<--- Score

68. Will there be any necessary staff changes (redundancies or new hires)?
<--- Score

69. What is something you believe that nearly no one agrees with you on?
<--- Score

70. Are new benefits received and understood?
<--- Score

71. Are you maintaining a past–present–future perspective throughout the Data communication discussion?
<--- Score

72. How do you maintain Data communication's Integrity?
<--- Score

73. How do you cross-sell and up-sell your Data communication success?
<--- Score

74. Who will be responsible for deciding whether Data communication goes ahead or not after the initial investigations?
<--- Score

75. Is a Data communication breakthrough on the horizon?
<--- Score

76. What are the potential basics of Data communication fraud?
<--- Score

77. If you do not follow, then how to lead?
<--- Score

78. What happens if you do not have enough funding?
<--- Score

79. How will you insure seamless interoperability of Data communication moving forward?
<--- Score

80. What are you challenging?
<--- Score

81. In the past year, what have you done (or could you have done) to increase the accurate perception of your company/brand as ethical and honest?
<--- Score

82. What are specific Data communication rules to follow?
<--- Score

83. Ask yourself: how would you do this work if you only had one staff member to do it?
<--- Score

84. Who is the main stakeholder, with ultimate responsibility for driving Data communication forward?
<--- Score

85. Do you feel that more should be done in the Data communication area?
<--- Score

86. What threat is Data communication addressing?
<--- Score

87. What are the key enablers to make this Data communication move?
<--- Score

88. What new services of functionality will be implemented next with Data communication ?
<--- Score

89. Are you making progress, and are you making progress as Data communication leaders?
<--- Score

90. Do you see more potential in people than they do in themselves?
<--- Score

91. If you got fired and a new hire took your place, what would she do different?
<--- Score

92. Do you say no to customers for no reason?
<--- Score

93. What trouble can you get into?
<--- Score

94. What is a feasible sequencing of reform initiatives over time?
<--- Score

95. What role does communication play in the success or failure of a Data communication project?
<--- Score

96. Can you do all this work?

<--- Score

97. Operational - will it work?
<--- Score

98. If you had to leave your organization for a year and the only communication you could have with employees/colleagues was a single paragraph, what would you write?
<--- Score

99. What stupid rule would you most like to kill?
<--- Score

100. Is the impact that Data communication has shown?
<--- Score

101. If you had to rebuild your organization without any traditional competitive advantages (i.e., no killer technology, promising research, innovative product/service delivery model, etcetera), how would your people have to approach their work and collaborate together in order to create the necessary conditions for success?
<--- Score

102. What knowledge, skills and characteristics mark a good Data communication project manager?
<--- Score

103. Have benefits been optimized with all key stakeholders?
<--- Score

104. What are you trying to prove to yourself, and how

might it be hijacking your life and business success?
<--- Score

105. What is it like to work for you?
<--- Score

106. Can you break it down?
<--- Score

107. Are there any activities that you can take off your to do list?
<--- Score

108. What trophy do you want on your mantle?
<--- Score

109. Did your employees make progress today?
<--- Score

110. Would you rather sell to knowledgeable and informed customers or to uninformed customers?
<--- Score

111. Are you paying enough attention to the partners your company depends on to succeed?
<--- Score

112. Is maximizing Data communication protection the same as minimizing Data communication loss?
<--- Score

113. How do you keep the momentum going?
<--- Score

114. What is the kind of project structure that would be appropriate for your Data communication project,

should it be formal and complex, or can it be less formal and relatively simple?
<--- Score

115. How will you ensure you get what you expected?
<--- Score

116. Do you know who is a friend or a foe?
<--- Score

117. Who do you think the world wants your organization to be?
<--- Score

118. Are the assumptions believable and achievable?
<--- Score

119. How do you foster innovation?
<--- Score

120. Do Data communication rules make a reasonable demand on a users capabilities?
<--- Score

121. How do you make it meaningful in connecting Data communication with what users do day-to-day?
<--- Score

122. How do you provide a safe environment -physically and emotionally?
<--- Score

123. Are you using a design thinking approach and integrating Innovation, Data communication Experience, and Brand Value?
<--- Score

124. How do you set Data communication stretch targets and how do you get people to not only participate in setting these stretch targets but also that they strive to achieve these?
<--- Score

125. How do you govern and fulfill your societal responsibilities?
<--- Score

126. Why do and why don't your customers like your organization?
<--- Score

127. What Data communication skills are most important?
<--- Score

128. Who do we want your customers to become?
<--- Score

129. What are your personal philosophies regarding Data communication and how do they influence your work?
<--- Score

130. How do you ensure that implementations of Data communication products are done in a way that ensures safety?
<--- Score

131. How will you motivate the stakeholders with the least vested interest?
<--- Score

132. How is implementation research currently incorporated into each of your goals?
<--- Score

133. How do you accomplish your long range Data communication goals?
<--- Score

134. Is your strategy driving your strategy? Or is the way in which you allocate resources driving your strategy?
<--- Score

135. Are all key stakeholders present at all Structured Walkthroughs?
<--- Score

136. Is Data communication dependent on the successful delivery of a current project?
<--- Score

137. Who are the key stakeholders?
<--- Score

138. Were lessons learned captured and communicated?
<--- Score

139. What will be the consequences to the stakeholder (financial, reputation etc) if Data communication does not go ahead or fails to deliver the objectives?
<--- Score

140. What is the overall business strategy?
<--- Score

141. What are your most important goals for the strategic Data communication objectives?
<--- Score

142. Why will customers want to buy your organizations products/services?
<--- Score

143. What have you done to protect your business from competitive encroachment?
<--- Score

144. How much does Data communication help?
<--- Score

145. How are you doing compared to your industry?
<--- Score

146. What are the short and long-term Data communication goals?
<--- Score

147. Do you have the right capabilities and capacities?
<--- Score

148. Are assumptions made in Data communication stated explicitly?
<--- Score

149. Can the schedule be done in the given time?
<--- Score

150. What are the success criteria that will indicate that Data communication objectives have been met and the benefits delivered?

<--- Score

151. Do you have enough freaky customers in your portfolio pushing you to the limit day in and day out?
<--- Score

152. Is it economical; do you have the time and money?
<--- Score

153. Is there any reason to believe the opposite of my current belief?
<--- Score

154. If you find that you havent accomplished one of the goals for one of the steps of the Data communication strategy, what will you do to fix it?
<--- Score

155. If you weren't already in this business, would you enter it today? And if not, what are you going to do about it?
<--- Score

156. Do you have past Data communication successes?
<--- Score

157. What are strategies for increasing support and reducing opposition?
<--- Score

158. What does your signature ensure?
<--- Score

159. At what moment would you think; Will I get fired?

<--- Score

160. What do we do when new problems arise?
<--- Score

161. What are the gaps in your knowledge and experience?
<--- Score

162. How do you stay inspired?
<--- Score

163. Why is it important to have senior management support for a Data communication project?
<--- Score

164. Who will manage the integration of tools?
<--- Score

165. Which functions and people interact with the supplier and or customer?
<--- Score

166. Who uses your product in ways you never expected?
<--- Score

167. What may be the consequences for the performance of an organization if all stakeholders are not consulted regarding Data communication?
<--- Score

168. Whom among your colleagues do you trust, and for what?
<--- Score

169. Who is responsible for Data communication?
<--- Score

170. What management system can you use to leverage the Data communication experience, ideas, and concerns of the people closest to the work to be done?
<--- Score

171. How much contingency will be available in the budget?
<--- Score

172. How do you know if you are successful?
<--- Score

173. What did you miss in the interview for the worst hire you ever made?
<--- Score

174. Is there any existing Data communication governance structure?
<--- Score

175. Why not do Data communication?
<--- Score

176. Political -is anyone trying to undermine this project?
<--- Score

177. Have new benefits been realized?
<--- Score

178. What is the purpose of Data communication in relation to the mission?

<--- Score

179. How do you foster the skills, knowledge, talents, attributes, and characteristics you want to have?
<--- Score

180. What are the long-term Data communication goals?
<--- Score

181. Who is on the team?
<--- Score

182. How do customers see your organization?
<--- Score

183. What is your Data communication strategy?
<--- Score

184. Are you changing as fast as the world around you?
<--- Score

185. What is the overall talent health of your organization as a whole at senior levels, and for each organization reporting to a member of the Senior Leadership Team?
<--- Score

186. To whom do you add value?
<--- Score

187. What are the challenges?
<--- Score

188. If you were responsible for initiating and

implementing major changes in your organization, what steps might you take to ensure acceptance of those changes?
<--- Score

189. Which individuals, teams or departments will be involved in Data communication?
<--- Score

190. What goals did you miss?
<--- Score

191. Instead of going to current contacts for new ideas, what if you reconnected with dormant contacts--the people you used to know? If you were going reactivate a dormant tie, who would it be?
<--- Score

192. Whose voice (department, ethnic group, women, older workers, etc) might you have missed hearing from in your company, and how might you amplify this voice to create positive momentum for your business?
<--- Score

193. What is your competitive advantage?
<--- Score

194. Is Data communication realistic, or are you setting yourself up for failure?
<--- Score

195. What would you recommend your friend do if he/she were facing this dilemma?
<--- Score

196. Is a Data communication team work effort in place?
<--- Score

197. If your company went out of business tomorrow, would anyone who doesn't get a paycheck here care?
<--- Score

198. Why is Data communication important for you now?
<--- Score

199. What are the rules and assumptions your industry operates under? What if the opposite were true?
<--- Score

200. How do you go about securing Data communication?
<--- Score

201. Who have you, as a company, historically been when you've been at your best?
<--- Score

202. Will it be accepted by users?
<--- Score

203. What counts that you are not counting?
<--- Score

204. Are you relevant? Will you be relevant five years from now? Ten?
<--- Score

205. How do you proactively clarify deliverables and Data communication quality expectations?

<--- Score

206. Which Data communication goals are the most important?
<--- Score

207. What is the big Data communication idea?
<--- Score

208. What should you stop doing?
<--- Score

Add up total points for this section:
_____ = Total points for this section

Divided by: ______ (number of statements answered) = ______ Average score for this section

Transfer your score to the Data communication Index at the beginning of the Self-Assessment.

# Data Communication and Managing Projects, Criteria for Project Managers:

# 1.0 Initiating Process Group: Data Communication

1. When must it be done?

2. What are the short and long term implications?

3. What were things that you did well, and could improve, and how?

4. Contingency planning. if a risk event occurs, what will you do?

5. What is the NEXT thing to do?

6. Although the Data Communication project manager does not directly manage procurement and contracting activities, who does manage procurement and contracting activities in your organization then if not the PM?

7. How can you make your needs known?

8. Were escalated issues resolved promptly?

9. Who supports, improves, and oversees standardized processes related to the Data Communication projects program?

10. What communication items need improvement?

11. Measurable - are the targets measurable?

12. What areas were overlooked on this Data Communication project?

13. What are the overarching issues of your organization?

14. What technical work to do in each phase?

15. How will you know you did it?

16. When will the Data Communication project be done?

17. What are the required resources?

18. Were sponsors and decision makers available when needed outside regularly scheduled meetings?

19. Where must it be done?

20. Which six sigma dmaic phase focuses on why and how defects and errors occur?

## 1.1 Project Charter: Data Communication

21. Why use a Data Communication project charter?

22. When is a charter needed?

23. What is the purpose of the Data Communication project?

24. Why do you manage integration?

25. What date will the task finish?

26. Does the Data Communication project need to consider any special capacity or capability issues?

27. Fit with other Products Compliments – Cannibalizes?

28. Who is the Data Communication project Manager?

29. How high should you set your goals?

30. Are there special technology requirements?

31. What are some examples of a business case?

32. Assumptions and constraints: what assumptions were made in defining the Data Communication project?

33. For whom?

34. Why Outsource?

35. What changes can you make to improve?

36. What does it need to do?

37. What barriers do you predict to your success?

38. How will you know that a change is an improvement?

39. What ideas do you have for initial tests of change (PDSA cycles)?

40. Why have you chosen the aim you have set forth?

## 1.2 Stakeholder Register: Data Communication

41. What & Why?

42. How should employers make voices heard?

43. How big is the gap?

44. How will reports be created?

45. What opportunities exist to provide communications?

46. Who wants to talk about Security?

47. How much influence do they have on the Data Communication project?

48. Who is managing stakeholder engagement?

49. What are the major Data Communication project milestones requiring communications or providing communications opportunities?

50. Is your organization ready for change?

51. What is the power of the stakeholder?

52. Who are the stakeholders?

## 1.3 Stakeholder Analysis Matrix: Data Communication

53. Why do you care?

54. Who will be responsible for managing the outcome?

55. Could any of your organizations weaknesses seriously threaten development?

56. Who holds positions of responsibility in interested organizations?

57. Price, value, quality?

58. Market developments?

59. Gaps in capabilities?

60. Do recommendations include actions to address any differential distribution of impacts?

61. Identify the stakeholders levels most frequently used -or at least sought- in your Data Communication projects and for which purpose?

62. How can you counter negative efforts?

63. What should thwe organizations stakeholders avoid?

64. Geographical, export, import?

65. What makes a person a stakeholder?

66. Who is influential in the Data Communication project area (both thematic and geographic areas)?

67. New technologies, services, ideas?

68. What is social & public accountability ?

69. Contributions to policy and practice?

70. Cultural, attitudinal, behavioural?

71. What are the reimbursement requirements?

72. Insurmountable weaknesses?

# 2.0 Planning Process Group: Data Communication

73. Are there efficient coordination mechanisms to avoid overloading the counterparts, participating stakeholders?

74. Who are the Data Communication project stakeholders?

75. Will the products created live up to the necessary quality?

76. How well do the team follow the chosen processes?

77. What business situation is being addressed?

78. Do the partners have sufficient financial capacity to keep up the benefits produced by the programme?

79. How can you tell when you are done?

80. Is the Data Communication project making progress in helping to achieve the set results?

81. What types of differentiated effects are resulting from the Data Communication project and to what extent?

82. How does activity resource estimation affect activity duration estimation?

83. How well did the chosen processes fit the needs of the Data Communication project?

84. How well defined and documented are the Data Communication project management processes you chose to use?

85. How do you integrate Data Communication project Planning with the Iterative/Evolutionary SDLC?

86. What do you need to do?

87. Professionals want to know what is expected from them; what are the deliverables?

88. To what extent are the visions and actions of the partners consistent or divergent with regard to the program?

89. Are the necessary foundations in place to ensure the sustainability of the results of the Data Communication project?

## 2.1 Project Management Plan: Data Communication

90. When is the Data Communication project management plan created?

91. What went wrong?

92. What if, for example, the positive direction and vision of your organization causes expected trends to change resulting in greater need than expected?

93. What goes into your Data Communication project Charter?

94. Is mitigation authorized or recommended?

95. How can you best help your organization to develop consistent practices in Data Communication project management planning stages?

96. What is Data Communication project scope management?

97. Are the proposed Data Communication project purposes different than a previously authorized Data Communication project?

98. Is the engineering content at a feasibility level-of-detail, and is it sufficiently complete, to provide an adequate basis for the baseline cost estimate?

99. Are there any scope changes proposed for a

previously authorized Data Communication project?

100. Will you add a schedule and diagram?

101. How do you organize the costs in the Data Communication project management plan?

102. What are the training needs?

103. Is there an incremental analysis/cost effectiveness analysis of proposed mitigation features based on an approved method and using an accepted model?

104. How do you manage integration?

105. What would you do differently what did not work?

106. Are alternatives safe, functional, constructible, economical, reasonable and sustainable?

107. What are the constraints?

108. What are the assumptions?

## 2.2 Scope Management Plan: Data Communication

109. Are schedule deliverables actually delivered?

110. Is there any form of automated support for Issues Management?

111. Where do scope management processes fit in?

112. Are written status reports provided on a designated frequent basis?

113. Is each item clearly and completely defined?

114. Are the Data Communication project plans updated on a frequent basis?

115. Is there an onboarding process in place?

116. Have Data Communication project success criteria been defined?

117. Has a proper Data Communication project work location been established that will allow the team to work together with user personnel?

118. Are stakeholders aware and supportive of the principles and practices of modern software estimation?

119. What weaknesses do you have?

120. Are changes in deliverable commitments agreed to by all affected groups & individuals?

121. What went right?

122. Is there a formal set of procedures supporting Issues Management?

123. Has the business need been clearly defined?

124. The greatest degree of uncertainty is encountered during which phase of the Data Communication project life cycle?

125. Has the budget been baselined?

126. Are the appropriate IT resources adequate to meet planned commitments?

127. Do you have the reasons why the changes to your organizational systems and capabilities are required?

## 2.3 Requirements Management Plan: Data Communication

128. Is any organizational data being used or stored?

129. How will unresolved questions be handled once approval has been obtained?

130. Will you perform a Requirements Risk assessment and develop a plan to deal with risks?

131. Will you document changes to requirements?

132. Do you have an agreed upon process for alerting the Data Communication project Manager if a request for change in requirements leads to a product scope change?

133. What is a problem?

134. Who is responsible for monitoring and tracking the Data Communication project requirements?

135. Will the product release be stable and mature enough to be deployed in the user community?

136. Is the system software (non-operating system) new to the IT Data Communication project team?

137. How detailed should the Data Communication project get?

138. When and how will a requirements baseline be

established in this Data Communication project?

139. What information regarding the Data Communication project requirements will be reported?

140. Did you get proper approvals?

141. Is it new or replacing an existing business system or process?

142. Did you distinguish the scope of work the contractor(s) will be required to do?

143. Has the requirements team been instructed in the Change Control process?

144. Does the Data Communication project have a Change Control process?

145. How knowledgeable is the primary Stakeholder(s) in the proposed application area?

146. In case of software development; Should you have a test for each code module?

147. What are you counting on?

## 2.4 Requirements Documentation: Data Communication

148. What if the system wasn t implemented?

149. What is a show stopper in the requirements?

150. Who is interacting with the system?

151. How linear / iterative is your Requirements Gathering process (or will it be)?

152. How will requirements be documented and who signs off on them?

153. What marketing channels do you want to use: e-mail, letter or sms?

154. Are all functions required by the customer included?

155. What happens when requirements are wrong?

156. Is the origin of the requirement clearly stated?

157. What is the risk associated with the technology?

158. What are the attributes of a customer?

159. How will the proposed Data Communication project help?

160. How much does requirements engineering cost?

161. What facilities must be supported by the system?

162. What images does it conjure?

163. Is your business case still valid?

164. If applicable; are there issues linked with the fact that this is an offshore Data Communication project?

165. Are there legal issues?

166. What kind of entity is a problem ?

167. How will they be documented / shared?

## 2.5 Requirements Traceability Matrix: Data Communication

168. How will it affect the stakeholders personally in career?

169. How small is small enough?

170. Is there a requirements traceability process in place?

171. Describe the process for approving requirements so they can be added to the traceability matrix and Data Communication project work can be performed. Will the Data Communication project requirements become approved in writing?

172. Why do you manage scope?

173. Will you use a Requirements Traceability Matrix?

174. How do you manage scope?

175. Why use a WBS?

176. Do you have a clear understanding of all subcontracts in place?

177. What are the chronologies, contingencies, consequences, criteria?

178. What is the WBS?

179. What percentage of Data Communication projects are producing traceability matrices between requirements and other work products?

## 2.6 Project Scope Statement: Data Communication

180. Risks?

181. Is your organization structure appropriate for the Data Communication projects size and complexity?

182. Is this process communicated to the customer and team members?

183. If there are vendors, have they signed off on the Data Communication project Plan?

184. Identify how your team and you will create the Data Communication project scope statement and the work breakdown structure (WBS). Document how you will create the Data Communication project scope statement and WBS, and make sure you answer the following questions: In defining Data Communication project scope and the WBS, will you and your Data Communication project team be using methods defined by your organization, methods defined by the Data Communication project management office (PMO), or other methods?

185. Is the scope of your Data Communication project well defined?

186. Is there a Quality Assurance Plan documented and filed?

187. Is the Data Communication project organization

documented and on file?

188. Has everyone approved the Data Communication projects scope statement?

189. Elements that deal with providing the detail?

190. If the scope changes, what will the impact be to your Data Communication project in terms of duration, cost, quality, or any other important areas of the Data Communication project?

191. How will you verify the accuracy of the work of the Data Communication project, and what constitutes acceptance of the deliverables?

192. Have the reports to be produced, distributed, and filed been defined?

193. Is the Data Communication project manager qualified and experienced in Data Communication project management?

194. How often will scope changes be reviewed?

195. Data Communication project lead, team lead, solution architect?

196. Will all Data Communication project issues be unconditionally tracked through the issue resolution process?

197. Will the Data Communication project risks be managed according to the Data Communication projects risk management process?

198. Are the meetings set up to have assigned note takers that will add action/issues to the issue list?

## 2.7 Assumption and Constraint Log: Data Communication

199. Are there cosmetic errors that hinder readability and comprehension?

200. Are there processes defining how software will be developed including development methods, overall timeline for development, software product standards, and traceability?

201. Is this model reasonable?

202. Are formal code reviews conducted?

203. Have all involved stakeholders and work groups committed to the Data Communication project?

204. If appropriate, is the deliverable content consistent with current Data Communication project documents and in compliance with the Document Management Plan?

205. Have you eliminated all duplicative tasks or manual efforts, where appropriate?

206. Has the approach and development strategy of the Data Communication project been defined, documented and accepted by the appropriate stakeholders?

207. Contradictory information between different documents?

208. Have adequate resources been provided by management to ensure Data Communication project success?

209. When can log be discarded?

210. What strengths do you have?

211. Does the plan conform to standards?

212. Should factors be unpredictable over time?

213. Is the current scope of the Data Communication project substantially different than that originally defined in the approved Data Communication project plan?

214. Have all stakeholders been identified?

215. Are there unnecessary steps that are creating bottlenecks and/or causing people to wait?

216. After observing execution of process, is it in compliance with the documented Plan?

## 2.8 Work Breakdown Structure: Data Communication

217. When does it have to be done?

218. How will you and your Data Communication project team define the Data Communication projects scope and work breakdown structure?

219. Where does it take place?

220. Is it still viable?

221. Can you make it?

222. Why would you develop a Work Breakdown Structure?

223. What has to be done?

224. Is the work breakdown structure (wbs) defined and is the scope of the Data Communication project clear with assigned deliverable owners?

225. Do you need another level?

226. How far down?

227. When do you stop?

228. Who has to do it?

229. Is it a change in scope?

230. How big is a work-package?

231. How many levels?

232. Why is it useful?

233. When would you develop a Work Breakdown Structure?

## 2.9 WBS Dictionary: Data Communication

234. Are significant decision points, constraints, and interfaces identified as key milestones?

235. Do work packages consist of discrete tasks which are adequately described?

236. Are your organizations and items of cost assigned to each pool identified?

237. Evaluate the performance of operating organizations?

238. Are overhead cost budgets established for each organization which has authority to incur overhead costs?

239. How much detail?

240. Are data elements summarized through the functional organizational structure for progressively higher levels of management?

241. Is cost and schedule performance measurement done in a consistent, systematic manner?

242. Are records maintained to show how management reserves are used?

243. Budgets assigned to control accounts?

244. Do procedures specify under what circumstances replanning of open work packages may occur, and the methods to be followed?

245. Are overhead budgets and costs being handled according to the disclosure statement when applicable, or otherwise properly classified (for example, engineering overhead, IR&D)?

246. Actual cost of work performed?

247. Does the contractor have procedures which permit identification of recurring or non-recurring costs as necessary?

248. Are overhead costs budgets established on a basis consistent with anticipated direct business base?

249. Does the accounting system provide a basis for auditing records of direct costs chargeable to the contract?

250. All cwbs elements specified for external reporting?

251. Are retroactive changes to direct costs and indirect costs prohibited except for the correction of errors and routine accounting adjustments?

252. Is all contract work included in the CWBS?

## 2.10 Schedule Management Plan: Data Communication

253. Has the scope management document been updated and distributed to help prevent scope creep?

254. Which status reports are received per the Data Communication project Plan?

255. Do all stakeholders know how to access this repository and where to find the Data Communication project documentation?

256. Have stakeholder accountabilities & responsibilities been clearly defined?

257. Does the ims include all contract and/or designated management control milestones?

258. Has a resource management plan been created?

259. Is there a formal set of procedures supporting Stakeholder Management?

260. Perform reality checks on schedules – are all tasks included?

261. Is an industry recognized mechanized support tool(s) being used for Data Communication project scheduling & tracking?

262. Are action items captured and managed?

263. Does the ims reflect accurate current status and credible start/finish forecasts for all to-go tasks and milestones?

264. Are risk oriented checklists used during risk identification?

265. Cost / benefit analysis?

266. Is the critical path valid?

267. Are multiple estimation methods being employed?

268. Are software metrics formally captured, analyzed and used as a basis for other Data Communication project estimates?

269. Are Data Communication project contact logs kept up to date?

270. Is your organization certified as a broker of the products/supplies?

271. Are all payments made according to the contract(s)?

## 2.11 Activity List: Data Communication

272. Can you determine the activity that must finish, before this activity can start?

273. What is the probability the Data Communication project can be completed in xx weeks?

274. Who will perform the work?

275. What are the critical bottleneck activities?

276. How much slack is available in the Data Communication project?

277. How will it be performed?

278. How detailed should a Data Communication project get?

279. Is infrastructure setup part of your Data Communication project?

280. What went well?

281. Where will it be performed?

282. What is your organizations history in doing similar activities?

283. How can the Data Communication project be displayed graphically to better visualize the activities?

284. What is the LF and LS for each activity?

285. Is there anything planned that does not need to be here?

286. How should ongoing costs be monitored to try to keep the Data Communication project within budget?

287. Should you include sub-activities?

288. How difficult will it be to do specific activities on this Data Communication project?

## 2.12 Activity Attributes: Data Communication

289. How many days do you need to complete the work scope with a limit of X number of resources?

290. Time for overtime?

291. How do you manage time?

292. Is there a trend during the year?

293. What activity do you think you should spend the most time on?

294. Where else does it apply?

295. How difficult will it be to do specific activities on this Data Communication project?

296. Can you re-assign any activities to another resource to resolve an over-allocation?

297. Does your organization of the data change its meaning?

298. How many resources do you need to complete the work scope within a limit of X number of days?

299. Were there other ways you could have organized the data to achieve similar results?

300. Resources to accomplish the work?

301. Would you consider either of corresponding activities an outlier?

302. Are the required resources available or need to be acquired?

303. Activity: what is In the Bag?

304. What is missing?

305. Has management defined a definite timeframe for the turnaround or Data Communication project window?

## 2.13 Milestone List: Data Communication

306. Describe your organizations strengths and core competencies. What factors will make your organization succeed?

307. Calculate how long can activity be delayed?

308. What has been done so far?

309. Vital contracts and partners?

310. Own known vulnerabilities?

311. What is the market for your technology, product or service?

312. What would happen if a delivery of material was one week late?

313. How will the milestone be verified?

314. Sustaining internal capabilities?

315. Information and research?

316. Milestone pages should display the UserID of the person who added the milestone. Does a report or query exist that provides this audit information?

317. Competitive advantages?

318. Can you derive how soon can the whole Data Communication project finish?

319. Usps (unique selling points)?

320. Legislative effects?

321. Effects on core activities, distraction?

## 2.14 Network Diagram: Data Communication

322. Where do you schedule uncertainty time?

323. If x is long, what would be the completion time if you break x into two parallel parts of y weeks and z weeks?

324. What job or jobs could run concurrently?

325. What can be done concurrently?

326. What controls the start and finish of a job?

327. If a current contract exists, can you provide the vendor name, contract start, and contract expiration date?

328. What activities must follow this activity?

329. What are the Major Administrative Issues?

330. What must be completed before an activity can be started?

331. What job or jobs follow it?

332. What job or jobs precede it?

333. How confident can you be in your milestone dates and the delivery date?

334. Exercise: what is the probability that the Data Communication project duration will exceed xx weeks?

335. What are the Key Success Factors?

336. Which type of network diagram allows you to depict four types of dependencies?

337. If the Data Communication project network diagram cannot change and you have extra personnel resources, what is the BEST thing to do?

338. Are the required resources available?

339. What are the tools?

340. Why must you schedule milestones, such as reviews, throughout the Data Communication project?

## 2.15 Activity Resource Requirements: Data Communication

341. When does monitoring begin?

342. Why do you do that?

343. Organizational Applicability?

344. Which logical relationship does the PDM use most often?

345. How do you handle petty cash?

346. Other support in specific areas?

347. What are constraints that you might find during the Human Resource Planning process?

348. What is the Work Plan Standard?

349. Do you use tools like decomposition and rolling-wave planning to produce the activity list and other outputs?

350. How many signatures do you require on a check and does this match what is in your policy and procedures?

351. Anything else?

352. Are there unresolved issues that need to be addressed?

## 2.16 Resource Breakdown Structure: Data Communication

353. Who will be used as a Data Communication project team member?

354. What can you do to improve productivity?

355. Why is this important?

356. How should the information be delivered?

357. What is the number one predictor of a groups productivity?

358. Which resources should be in the resource pool?

359. Who is allowed to see what data about which resources?

360. How can this help you with team building?

361. What defines a successful Data Communication project?

362. What are the requirements for resource data?

363. Any changes from stakeholders?

364. Why do you do it?

365. Changes based on input from stakeholders?

366. Who is allowed to perform which functions?

367. When do they need the information?

368. What is the purpose of assigning and documenting responsibility?

369. What is each stakeholders desired outcome for the Data Communication project?

## 2.17 Activity Duration Estimates: Data Communication

370. Are risks monitored to determine if an event has occurred or if the mitigation was successful?

371. Mass, power, cost ... why not time?

372. How can software assist in Data Communication project communications?

373. Why should Data Communication project managers strive to make jobs look easy?

374. What do corresponding sources say about Data Communication project management?

375. Are activity duration estimates documented?

376. Did anything besides luck make a difference between success and failure?

377. What are the three main outputs of quality control?

378. What type of activity sequencing method is required for corresponding activities?

379. What are the nine areas of expertise?

380. How is the Data Communication project doing?

381. What is the difference between % Complete and

% work?

382. What is the career outlook for Data Communication project managers in information technology?

383. Which type of mathematical analysis is being used?

384. List five reasons why organizations outsource. Why is there a growing trend in outsourcing, especially in the government?

385. What tasks can take place concurrently?

386. What are two suggestions for ensuring adequate change control on Data Communication projects that involve outside contracts?

387. Data Communication project manager is using weighted average duration estimates to perform schedule network analysis. Which type of mathematical analysis is being used?

388. What are crucial elements of successful Data Communication project plan execution?

## 2.18 Duration Estimating Worksheet: Data Communication

389. What work will be included in the Data Communication project?

390. When do the individual activities need to start and finish?

391. Is the Data Communication project responsive to community need?

392. Science = process: remember the scientific method?

393. What is next?

394. Value pocket identification & quantification what are value pockets?

395. How should ongoing costs be monitored to try to keep the Data Communication project within budget?

396. Why estimate costs?

397. What is an Average Data Communication project?

398. Done before proceeding with this activity or what can be done concurrently?

399. Why estimate time and cost?

400. What info is needed?

401. Does the Data Communication project provide innovative ways for stakeholders to overcome obstacles or deliver better outcomes?

402. Is a construction detail attached (to aid in explanation)?

403. When, then?

404. Small or large Data Communication project?

405. What is the total time required to complete the Data Communication project if no delays occur?

406. What utility impacts are there?

# 2.19 Project Schedule: Data Communication

407. How can you minimize or control changes to Data Communication project schedules?

408. What does that mean?

409. What is Data Communication project management?

410. Did the final product meet or exceed user expectations?

411. Did the Data Communication project come in under budget?

412. Data Communication project work estimates Who is managing the work estimate quality of work tasks in the Data Communication project schedule?

413. Change management required?

414. How can you fix it?

415. Have all Data Communication project delays been adequately accounted for, communicated to all stakeholders and adjustments made in overall Data Communication project schedule?

416. How much slack is available in the Data Communication project?

417. How closely did the initial Data Communication project Schedule compare with the actual schedule?

418. How does a Data Communication project get to be a year late ?

419. How effectively were issues able to be resolved without impacting the Data Communication project Schedule or Budget?

420. Are all remaining durations correct?

421. Month Data Communication project take?

422. How can you shorten the schedule?

423. Are there activities that came from a template or previous Data Communication project that are not applicable on this phase of this Data Communication project?

424. What documents, if any, will the subcontractor provide (eg Data Communication project schedule, quality plan etc)?

425. Understand the constraints used in preparing the schedule. Are activities connected because logic dictates the order in which others occur?

## 2.20 Cost Management Plan: Data Communication

426. Schedule contingency – how will the schedule contingency be administrated?

427. Have reserves been created to address risks?

428. Timeline and milestones?

429. Has a provision been made to reassess Data Communication project risks at various Data Communication project stages?

430. Scope of work – What is the scope of work for each of the planned contracts?

431. Were Data Communication project team members involved in the development of activity & task decomposition?

432. How does the proposed individual meet each requirement?

433. Technical and functional?

434. Are Data Communication project team members committed fulltime?

435. Are key risk mitigation strategies added to the Data Communication project schedule?

436. What threats might prevent you from getting

there?

437. Cost tracking and performance analysis – How will cost tracking and performance analysis be accomplished?

438. Is there general agreement & acceptance of the current status and progress of the Data Communication project?

439. Is the communication plan being followed?

440. Are all vendor contracts closed out?

441. Have all involved Data Communication project stakeholders and work groups committed to the Data Communication project?

442. Mitigation – based on the action, cost and probability of success, will the mitigation be made?

443. Have process improvement efforts been completed before requirements efforts begin?

444. Are internal Data Communication project status meetings held at reasonable intervals?

445. Is there anything unique in this Data Communication projects scope statement that will affect resources?

## 2.21 Activity Cost Estimates: Data Communication

446. Were the tasks or work products prepared by the consultant useful?

447. What is your organizations history in doing similar tasks?

448. The impact and what actions were taken?

449. What is procurement?

450. What is the estimators estimating history?

451. Where can you get activity reports?

452. Can you delete activities or make them inactive?

453. What defines a successful Data Communication project?

454. How do you do activity recasts?

455. Performance bond should always provide what part of the contract value?

456. What were things that you did very well and want to do the same again on the next Data Communication project?

457. What areas does the group agree are the biggest success on the Data Communication project?

458. Estimated cost?

459. How difficult will it be to do specific tasks on the Data Communication project?

460. Does the estimator estimate by task or by person?

461. Would you hire them again?

462. What is the last item a Data Communication project manager must do to finalize Data Communication project close-out?

463. Vac -variance at completion, how much over/ under budget do you expect to be?

464. Can you change your activities?

## 2.22 Cost Estimating Worksheet: Data Communication

465. What is the estimated labor cost today based upon this information?

466. Is it feasible to establish a control group arrangement?

467. What happens to any remaining funds not used?

468. Ask: are others positioned to know, are others credible, and will others cooperate?

469. What costs are to be estimated?

470. Will the Data Communication project collaborate with the local community and leverage resources?

471. Does the Data Communication project provide innovative ways for stakeholders to overcome obstacles or deliver better outcomes?

472. What will others want?

473. What can be included?

474. Can a trend be established from historical performance data on the selected measure and are the criteria for using trend analysis or forecasting methods met?

475. What is the purpose of estimating?

476. What additional Data Communication project(s) could be initiated as a result of this Data Communication project?

477. How will the results be shared and to whom?

478. Is the Data Communication project responsive to community need?

479. Identify the timeframe necessary to monitor progress and collect data to determine how the selected measure has changed?

480. Who is best positioned to know and assist in identifying corresponding factors?

## 2.23 Cost Baseline: Data Communication

481. Has the documentation relating to operation and maintenance of the product(s) or service(s) been delivered to, and accepted by, operations management?

482. Has operations management formally accepted responsibility for operating and maintaining the product(s) or service(s) delivered by the Data Communication project?

483. How will cost estimates be used?

484. What would the life cycle costs be?

485. Has training and knowledge transfer of the operations organization been completed?

486. Are you asking management for something as a result of this update?

487. Is request in line with priorities?

488. Is there anything you need from upper management in order to be successful?

489. Impact to environment?

490. Is there anything unique in this Data Communication projects scope statement that will affect resources?

491. Has the actual cost of the Data Communication project (or Data Communication project phase) been tallied and compared to the approved budget?

492. What deliverables come first?

493. Escalation criteria met?

494. If you sold 10x widgets on a day, what would the affect on profits be?

495. How accurate do cost estimates need to be?

496. Have the actual milestone completion dates been compared to the approved schedule?

497. Has the Data Communication project documentation been archived or otherwise disposed as described in the Data Communication project communication plan?

498. Will the Data Communication project fail if the change request is not executed?

## 2.24 Quality Management Plan: Data Communication

499. Are there trends or hot spots?

500. How are changes to procedures made?

501. Have Data Communication project management standards and procedures been established and documented?

502. Who else should be involved ?

503. Can you perform this task or activity in a more effective manner?

504. How does your organization maintain a safe and healthy work environment?

505. How do you prioritize?

506. What is quality planning ?

507. How are senior leaders, employees, and your organization involved in supporting the community?

508. Does the program use other agents to collect samples?

509. How does your organization design processes to ensure others meet customer and others requirements?

510. How do senior leaders create your organizational focus on customers and other stakeholders?

511. How are calibration records kept?

512. How long do you retain data?

513. Are best practices and metrics employed to identify issues, progress, performance, etc.?

514. Show/provide copy of procedures for taking field notes?

515. How do you decide who is responsible for signing the data reports?

516. Are you meeting your customers expectations consistently?

517. What is quality and how will you ensure it?

## 2.25 Quality Metrics: Data Communication

518. What method of measurement do you use?

519. How does one achieve stability?

520. Was review conducted per standard protocols?

521. Who notifies stakeholders of normal and abnormal results?

522. Was the overall quality better or worse than previous products?

523. What group is empowered to define quality requirements?

524. Subjective quality component: customer satisfaction, how do you measure it?

525. Did evaluation start on time?

526. How do you calculate such metrics?

527. What documentation is required?

528. Which are the right metrics to use?

529. There are many reasons to shore up quality-related metrics, and what metrics are important?

530. What level of statistical confidence do you use?

531. Is quality culture a competitive advantage?

532. How do you calculate corresponding metrics?

533. Is there alignment within your organization on definitions?

534. The metrics–what is being considered?

535. Filter visualizations of interest?

536. Are quality metrics defined?

537. What is the CMS Benchmark?

## 2.26 Process Improvement Plan: Data Communication

538. Are you making progress on your improvement plan?

539. Are you following the quality standards?

540. Have storage and access mechanisms and procedures been determined?

541. Purpose of goal: the motive is determined by asking, why do you want to achieve this goal?

542. Are you making progress on the improvement framework?

543. Why do you want to achieve the goal?

544. Have the frequency of collection and the points in the process where measurements will be made been determined?

545. Where do you want to be?

546. Where are you now?

547. Has a process guide to collect the data been developed?

548. What makes people good SPI coaches?

549. Are you making progress on the goals?

550. What is the test-cycle concept?

551. Does your process ensure quality?

552. What personnel are the champions for the initiative?

553. Who should prepare the process improvement action plan?

554. What actions are needed to address the problems and achieve the goals?

555. Everyone agrees on what process improvement is, right?

556. How do you measure?

557. Why quality management?

## 2.27 Responsibility Assignment Matrix: Data Communication

558. How do you assist them to be as productive as possible?

559. What are some important Data Communication project communications management tools?

560. What are the deliverables?

561. Does each role with Accountable responsibility have the authority within your organization to make the required decisions?

562. Too many is: do all the identified roles need to be routinely informed or only in exceptional circumstances?

563. Does the contractors system identify work accomplishment against the schedule plan?

564. The anticipated business volume?

565. Too many as: does a proper segregation of duties exist?

566. Availability – will the group or the person be available within the necessary time interval?

567. What simple tool can you use to help identify and prioritize Data Communication project risks that is very low tech and high touch?

568. Who is responsible for work and budgets for each wbs?

569. Who is the Data Communication project Manager?

570. Who is going to do that work?

571. Are people encouraged to bring up issues?

572. What do you do when people do not respond?

573. Performance to date and material commitment?

574. Undistributed budgets, if any?

## 2.28 Roles and Responsibilities: Data Communication

575. What should you do now to ensure that you are meeting all expectations of your current position?

576. Do you take the time to clearly define roles and responsibilities on Data Communication project tasks?

577. Who is responsible for each task?

578. Who: who is involved?

579. Are your budgets supportive of a culture of quality data?

580. Attainable / achievable: the goal is attainable; can you actually accomplish the goal?

581. What areas of supervision are challenging for you?

582. Is feedback clearly communicated and non-judgmental?

583. Is there a training program in place for stakeholders covering expectations, roles and responsibilities and any addition knowledge others need to be good stakeholders?

584. Was the expectation clearly communicated?

585. Once the responsibilities are defined for the Data Communication project, have the deliverables, roles and responsibilities been clearly communicated to every participant?

586. What expectations were NOT met?

587. What is working well?

588. Have you ever been a part of this team?

589. Are Data Communication project team roles and responsibilities identified and documented?

590. What are your major roles and responsibilities in the area of performance measurement and assessment?

591. Key conclusions and recommendations: Are conclusions and recommendations relevant and acceptable?

592. Are Data Communication project team roles and responsibilities identified and documented?

593. To decide whether to use a quality measurement, ask how will you know when it is achieved?

## 2.29 Human Resource Management Plan: Data Communication

594. List roles. what commitments have been made?

595. Are the quality tools and methods identified in the Quality Plan appropriate to the Data Communication project?

596. Have all involved Data Communication project stakeholders and work groups committed to the Data Communication project?

597. Has a sponsor been identified?

598. Is pert / critical path or equivalent methodology being used?

599. What areas does the group agree are the biggest success on the Data Communication project?

600. Responsiveness to change and the resulting demands for different skills and abilities?

601. Does the Data Communication project have a formal Data Communication project Charter?

602. Are change requests logged and managed?

603. Is documentation created for communication with the suppliers and Vendors?

604. How to convince employees that this is a

necessary process?

605. Were Data Communication project team members involved in the development of activity & task decomposition?

606. Are there checklists created to determine if all quality processes are followed?

607. What did you have to assume to be true to complete the charter?

608. Who will be impacted (both positively and negatively) as a result of or during the execution of this Data Communication project?

609. List the assumptions made to date. What did you have to assume to be true to complete the charter?

610. Is Data Communication project work proceeding in accordance with the original Data Communication project schedule?

## 2.30 Communications Management Plan: Data Communication

611. Who are the members of the governing body?

612. What help do you and your team need from the stakeholder?

613. Do you prepare stakeholder engagement plans?

614. Are the stakeholders getting the information others need, are others consulted, are concerns addressed?

615. Why manage stakeholders?

616. How often do you engage with stakeholders?

617. How much time does it take to do it?

618. What approaches to you feel are the best ones to use?

619. Who to learn from?

620. Are there potential barriers between the team and the stakeholder?

621. What to know?

622. Why do you manage communications?

623. What data is going to be required?

624. Which team member will work with each stakeholder?

625. Do you have members of your team responsible for certain stakeholders?

626. Are there common objectives between the team and the stakeholder?

627. Are stakeholders internal or external?

628. Are others needed?

629. Who is the stakeholder?

## 2.31 Risk Management Plan: Data Communication

630. Where are you confronted with risks during the business phases?

631. Financial risk: can your organization afford to undertake the Data Communication project?

632. What is the likelihood that your organization would accept responsibility for the risk?

633. How much risk protection can you afford?

634. Risk probability and impact: how will the probabilities and impacts of risk items be assessed?

635. Have top software and customer managers formally committed to support the Data Communication project?

636. Do requirements demand the use of new analysis, design, or testing methods?

637. Internal technical and management reviews?

638. How are risk analvsis and prioritization performed?

639. How is the audit profession changing?

640. How will the Data Communication project know if your organizations risk response actions were

effective?

641. Are flexibility and reuse paramount?

642. What are it-specific requirements?

643. Does the customer have a solid idea of what is required?

644. Is the process being followed?

645. What can go wrong?

646. Who/what can assist?

647. What will the damage be?

648. Why do you want risk management?

649. Number of users of the product?

## 2.32 Risk Register: Data Communication

650. What are the assumptions and current status that support the assessment of the risk?

651. Preventative actions - planned actions to reduce the likelihood a risk will occur and/or reduce the seriousness should it occur. What should you do now?

652. What should you do when?

653. Assume the event happens, what is the Most Likely impact?

654. What further options might be available for responding to the risk?

655. Recovery actions - planned actions taken once a risk has occurred to allow you to move on. What should you do after?

656. How well are risks controlled?

657. Risk documentation: what reporting formats and processes will be used for risk management activities?

658. How often will the Risk Management Plan and Risk Register be formally reviewed, and by whom?

659. What are the main aims, objectives of the policy, strategy, or service and the intended outcomes?

660. What may happen or not go according to plan?

661. When will it happen?

662. What evidence do you have to justify the likelihood score of the risk (audit, incident report, claim, complaints, inspection, internal review)?

663. Are your objectives at risk?

664. What should the audit role be in establishing a risk management process?

665. Why would you develop a risk register?

666. What will be done?

667. Schedule impact/severity estimated range (workdays) assume the event happens, what is the potential impact?

## 2.33 Probability and Impact Assessment: Data Communication

668. Who should be notified of the occurrence of each of the risk indicators?

669. Are the risk data timely and relevant?

670. Are the facilities, expertise, resources, and management know-how available to handle the situation?

671. Management -what contingency plans do you have if the risk becomes a reality?

672. What are the chances the risk event will occur?

673. What can you do about it?

674. What action do you usually take against risks?

675. Is the process supported by tools?

676. What should be the level of difficulty in handling the technology?

677. What new technologies are being explored in the same area?

678. Do you have a mechanism for managing change?

679. What risks does the employee encounter?

680. How would you assess the risk management process in the Data Communication project?

681. Is the present organizational structure for handling the Data Communication project sufficient?

682. How do risks change during a Data Communication project life cycle?

683. What is the impact if the risk does occur?

684. Risk categorization -which of your categories has more risk than others?

685. Are tool mentors available?

686. What are the levels of understanding of the future users of the outcome/results of this Data Communication project?

## 2.34 Probability and Impact Matrix: Data Communication

687. What are the chances the event will occur?

688. Is the present organizational structure for handling the Data Communication project sufficient?

689. Can it be changed quickly?

690. Can you avoid altogether some things that might go wrong?

691. Are you working on the right risks?

692. What should be the gestation period for the Data Communication project with this technology?

693. Is the Data Communication project cutting across the entire organization?

694. Risk may be made during which step of risk management?

695. What will be the impact or consequence if the risk occurs?

696. How much is the probability of the risk occurring?

697. Will there be an increase in the political conservatism?

698. Have customers been involved fully in the definition of requirements?

699. What did not work so well?

700. Are formal technical reviews part of this process?

701. How would you suggest monitoring for risk transition indicators?

702. Which is the BEST thing to do?

703. How solid is the Data Communication projection of competitive reaction?

704. Can it be enlarged by drawing people from other areas of your organization?

705. Which should be probably done NEXT?

706. What are the preparations required for facing difficulties?

## 2.35 Risk Data Sheet: Data Communication

707. What is the likelihood of it happening?

708. What will be the consequences if the risk happens?

709. If it happens, what are the consequences?

710. What actions can be taken to eliminate or remove risk?

711. Whom do you serve (customers)?

712. During work activities could hazards exist?

713. What will be the consequences if it happens?

714. What is the chance that it will happen?

715. Who has a vested interest in how you perform as your organization (our stakeholders)?

716. How can hazards be reduced?

717. Will revised controls lead to tolerable risk levels?

718. Are new hazards created?

719. What are you trying to achieve (Objectives)?

720. What are you weak at and therefore need to do

better?

721. What are the main opportunities available to you that you should grab while you can?

722. What if client refuses?

723. What are the main threats to your existence?

724. What are you here for (Mission)?

725. Has the most cost-effective solution been chosen?

726. What do you know?

## 2.36 Procurement Management Plan: Data Communication

727. Are issues raised, assessed, actioned, and resolved in a timely and efficient manner?

728. Is there a procurement management plan in place?

729. Is the structure for tracking the Data Communication project schedule well defined and assigned to a specific individual?

730. Have the key functions and capabilities been defined and assigned to each release or iteration?

731. Are vendor contract reports, reviews and visits conducted periodically?

732. Are the budget estimates reasonable?

733. Has a capability assessment been conducted?

734. Public engagement – did you get it right?

735. Is there an approved case?

736. Is there an issues management plan in place?

737. Is there a requirements change management processes in place?

738. How will you coordinate Procurement with

aspects of the Data Communication project?

739. Are all resource assumptions documented?

740. Are the quality tools and methods identified in the Quality Plan appropriate to the Data Communication project?

## 2.37 Source Selection Criteria: Data Communication

741. How can solicitation Schedules be improved to yield more effective price competition?

742. Who is entitled to a debriefing?

743. Do you want to wait until all offerors have been evaluated?

744. How do you encourage efficiency and consistency?

745. What should be considered?

746. What should a DRFP include?

747. Is this a cost contract?

748. What documentation is necessary regarding electronic communications?

749. What is the role of counsel in the procurement process?

750. What is the basis of an estimate and what assumptions were made?

751. Who is on the Source Selection Advisory Committee?

752. Can you prevent comparison of proposals?

753. Do you want to have them collaborate at subfactor level?

754. When is it appropriate to conduct a preproposal conference?

755. Are they compliant with all technical requirements?

756. What can not be disclosed?

757. What is price analysis and when should it be performed?

758. Are resultant proposal revisions allowed?

759. In which phase of the acquisition process cycle does source qualifications reside?

760. What aspects should the contracting officer brief the Data Communication project on prior to evaluation of proposals?

## 2.38 Stakeholder Management Plan: Data Communication

761. What training requirements are there based upon the required skills and resources?

762. Does the business case include how the Data Communication project aligns with your organizations strategic goals & objectives?

763. Have the procedures for identifying budget variances been followed?

764. Are mitigation strategies identified?

765. How will the equipment be verified?

766. What other teams / processes would be impacted by changes to the current process, and how?

767. Does the Data Communication project have a formal Data Communication project Plan?

768. Who would sign off on the charter?

769. Are the payment terms being followed?

770. Was the scope definition used in task sequencing?

771. Why would a customer be interested in a particular product or service?

772. What are reporting requirements?

773. Have Data Communication project team accountabilities & responsibilities been clearly defined?

774. Was trending evident between reviews?

775. Are corrective actions and variances reported?

776. Is the quality assurance team identified?

## 2.39 Change Management Plan: Data Communication

777. Will you need new processes?

778. What are the specific target groups/audiences that will be impacted by this change?

779. Who might present the most resistance?

780. What relationships will change?

781. What are the current methods of sharing information and do there need to be new ones developed?

782. Why is the initiative is being undertaken - What are the business drivers?

783. Who will be the change levers?

784. What can you do to minimise misinterpretation and negative perceptions?

785. What are the major changes to processes?

786. What is the reason for the communication?

787. Readiness -what is a successful end state?

788. What does a resilient organization look like?

789. What will be the preferred method of delivery?

790. Would you need to tailor a special message for each segment of the audience?

791. Will the readiness criteria be met prior to the training roll out?

792. What is the worst thing that can happen if you communicate information?

793. Do you need a new organizational structure?

794. Is there an adequate supply of people for the new roles?

795. Have the business unit contacts been briefed by the Data Communication project team?

# 3.0 Executing Process Group: Data Communication

796. What are the main parts of the scope statement?

797. What is the difference between conceptual, application, and evaluative questions?

798. What are deliverables of your Data Communication project?

799. Are decisions made in a timely manner?

800. Does software appear easy to learn?

801. How can you use Microsoft Data Communication project and Excel to assist in Data Communication project risk management?

802. Does the Data Communication project team have enough people to execute the Data Communication project plan?

803. What are the main processes included in Data Communication project quality management?

804. How will professionals learn what is expected from them what the deliverables are?

805. What are the critical steps involved in selecting measures and initiatives?

806. Will new hardware or software be required for

servers or client machines?

807. Why do you need a good WBS to use Data Communication project management software?

808. How does the job market and current state of the economy affect human resource management?

809. Is the schedule for the set products being met?

810. What are the critical steps involved with strategy mapping?

811. How can software assist in procuring goods and services?

812. Why is it important to determine activity sequencing on Data Communication projects?

813. How do you control progress of your Data Communication project?

## 3.1 Team Member Status Report: Data Communication

814. How does this product, good, or service meet the needs of the Data Communication project and your organization as a whole?

815. Does your organization have the means (staff, money, contract, etc.) to produce or to acquire the product, good, or service?

816. The problem with Reward & Recognition Programs is that the truly deserving people all too often get left out. How can you make it practical?

817. Are your organizations Data Communication projects more successful over time?

818. Does the product, good, or service already exist within your organization?

819. Is there evidence that staff is taking a more professional approach toward management of your organizations Data Communication projects?

820. How much risk is involved?

821. Why is it to be done?

822. How can you make it practical?

823. What is to be done?

824. How it is to be done?

825. Are the products of your organizations Data Communication projects meeting customers objectives?

826. Does every department have to have a Data Communication project Manager on staff?

827. How will resource planning be done?

828. Do you have an Enterprise Data Communication project Management Office (EPMO)?

829. Are the attitudes of staff regarding Data Communication project work improving?

830. When a teams productivity and success depend on collaboration and the efficient flow of information, what generally fails them?

831. What specific interest groups do you have in place?

832. Will the staff do training or is that done by a third party?

## 3.2 Change Request: Data Communication

833. Have all related configuration items been properly updated?

834. How does a team identify the discrete elements of a configuration?

835. Will all change requests and current status be logged?

836. How are the measures for carrying out the change established?

837. What is the change request log?

838. How does your organization control changes before and after software is released to a customer?

839. Does the schedule include Data Communication project management time and change request analysis time?

840. Why were your requested changes rejected or not made?

841. What kind of information about the change request needs to be captured?

842. What is a Change Request Form?

843. Customer acceptance plan how will the

customer verify the change has been implemented successfully?

844. What should be regulated in a change control operating instruction?

845. Screen shots or attachments included in a Change Request?

846. Have scm procedures for noting the change, recording it, and reporting it been followed?

847. Who is responsible to authorize changes?

848. What is the function of the change control committee?

849. What mechanism is used to appraise others of changes that are made?

850. Has the change been highlighted and documented in the CSCI?

851. How shall the implementation of changes be recorded?

852. Has a formal technical review been conducted to assess technical correctness?

## 3.3 Change Log: Data Communication

853. Is the change backward compatible without limitations?

854. How does this change affect scope?

855. Is the submitted change a new change or a modification of a previously approved change?

856. How does this relate to the standards developed for specific business processes?

857. Is this a mandatory replacement?

858. Does the suggested change request represent a desired enhancement to the products functionality?

859. Is the change request within Data Communication project scope?

860. Do the described changes impact on the integrity or security of the system?

861. Where do changes come from?

862. How does this change affect the timeline of the schedule?

863. Does the suggested change request seem to represent a necessary enhancement to the product?

864. Will the Data Communication project fail if the change request is not executed?

865. Is the change request open, closed or pending?

866. When was the request submitted?

867. When was the request approved?

868. Who initiated the change request?

869. Should a more thorough impact analysis be conducted?

870. Is the requested change request a result of changes in other Data Communication project(s)?

## 3.4 Decision Log: Data Communication

871. What is your overall strategy for quality control / quality assurance procedures?

872. It becomes critical to track and periodically revisit both operational effectiveness; Are you noticing all that you need to, and are you interpreting what you see effectively?

873. What makes you different or better than others companies selling the same thing?

874. What was the rationale for the decision?

875. Which variables make a critical difference?

876. How does the use a Decision Support System influence the strategies/tactics or costs?

877. Behaviors; what are guidelines that the team has identified that will assist them with getting the most out of team meetings?

878. Linked to original objective?

879. Who is the decisionmaker?

880. What eDiscovery problem or issue did your organization set out to fix or make better?

881. How do you know when you are achieving it?

882. Does anything need to be adjusted?

883. What is the line where eDiscovery ends and document review begins?

884. How does an increasing emphasis on cost containment influence the strategies and tactics used?

885. Decision-making process; how will the team make decisions?

886. What alternatives/risks were considered?

887. Adversarial environment. is your opponent open to a non-traditional workflow, or will it likely challenge anything you do?

888. Is your opponent open to a non-traditional workflow, or will it likely challenge anything you do?

889. Is everything working as expected?

890. With whom was the decision shared or considered?

## 3.5 Quality Audit: Data Communication

891. How does your organization know that its research programs are appropriately effective and constructive?

892. How does your organization know that its relationships with relevant professional bodies are appropriately effective and constructive?

893. Statements of intent remain exactly that until they are put into effect. The next step is to deploy the already stated intentions. In other words, do the plans happen in reality?

894. Are salvageable and salvaged medical devices stored in a manner to prevent damage and/or contamination?

895. Does the supplier use a formal quality system?

896. Is progress against the intentions measurable?

897. What happens if your organization fails its Quality Audit?

898. How does your organization know that the range and quality of its social and recreational services and facilities are appropriately effective and constructive in meeting the needs of staff?

899. How does your organization know that it

provides a safe and healthy environment?

900. How does your organization know that the review processes are effective?

901. Are all employees including salespersons made aware that they must report all complaints received from any source for inclusion in the complaint handling system?

902. What does the organizarion look for in a Quality audit?

903. What does an analysis of your organizations staff profile suggest in terms of its planning, and how is this being addressed?

904. Is your organizational structure established and each positions responsibility defined?

905. Are there appropriate indicators for monitoring the effectiveness and efficiency of processes?

906. How are you auditing your organizations compliance with regulations?

907. How does your organization know that the range and quality of its accommodation, catering and transportation services are appropriately effective and constructive?

908. How does your organization know that the quality of its supervisors is appropriately effective and constructive?

909. How does your organization know that its

systems for assisting staff with career planning and employment placements are appropriately effective and constructive?

910. Is the continuing professional education of key personnel account fored in detail?

## 3.6 Team Directory: Data Communication

911. Decisions: is the most suitable form of contract being used?

912. Decisions: what could be done better to improve the quality of the constructed product?

913. Who will write the meeting minutes and distribute?

914. Is construction on schedule?

915. Process decisions: are contractors adequately prosecuting the work?

916. How and in what format should information be presented?

917. How will you accomplish and manage the objectives?

918. How does the team resolve conflicts and ensure tasks are completed?

919. Where should the information be distributed?

920. Who will be the stakeholders on your next Data Communication project?

921. Process decisions: which organizational elements and which individuals will be assigned management

functions?

922. Why is the work necessary?

923. What needs to be communicated?

924. Process decisions: how well was task order work performed?

925. Process decisions: do invoice amounts match accepted work in place?

926. Days from the time the issue is identified?

927. How will the team handle changes?

928. Process decisions: are there any statutory or regulatory issues relevant to the timely execution of work?

929. Who are your stakeholders (customers, sponsors, end users, team members)?

## 3.7 Team Operating Agreement: Data Communication

930. Did you recap the meeting purpose, time, and expectations?

931. What is teaming?

932. What is group supervision?

933. Do you record meetings for the already stated unable to attend?

934. What are the boundaries (organizational or geographic) within which you operate?

935. What is the number of cases currently teamed?

936. Conflict resolution: how will disputes and other conflicts be mediated or resolved?

937. The method to be used in the decision making process; Will it be consensus, majority rule, or the supervisor having the final say?

938. Do team members need to frequently communicate as a full group to make timely decisions?

939. What administrative supports will be put in place to support the team and the teams supervisor?

940. Must your team members rely on the expertise of

other members to complete tasks?

941. Does your team need access to all documents and information at all times?

942. Do you ask participants to close laptops and place mobile devices on silent on the table while the meeting is in progress?

943. What is a Virtual Team?

944. Do you brief absent members after they view meeting notes or listen to a recording?

945. What is your unique contribution to your organization?

946. Communication protocols: how will the team communicate?

947. Do you begin with a question to engage everyone?

948. Do you call or email participants to ensure understanding, follow-through and commitment to the meeting outcomes?

949. How will you divide work equitably?

## 3.8 Team Performance Assessment: Data Communication

950. How hard do you try to make a good selection?

951. To what degree does the teams purpose contain themes that are particularly meaningful and memorable?

952. What are you doing specifically to develop the leaders around you?

953. Do friends perform better than acquaintances?

954. To what degree can all members engage in open and interactive considerations?

955. How much interpersonal friction is there in your team?

956. Where to from here?

957. To what degree are staff involved as partners in the improvement process?

958. Social categorization and intergroup behaviour: Does minimal intergroup discrimination make social identity more positive?

959. When a reviewer complains about method variance, what is the essence of the complaint?

960. When does the medium matter?

961. How does Data Communication project termination impact Data Communication project team members?

962. To what degree do all members feel responsible for all agreed-upon measures?

963. How do you recognize and praise members for contributions?

964. To what degree do team members frequently explore the teams purpose and its implications?

965. To what degree can team members meet frequently enough to accomplish the teams ends?

966. To what degree does the teams purpose constitute a broader, deeper aspiration than just accomplishing short-term goals?

967. To what degree does the teams work approach provide opportunity for members to engage in fact-based problem solving?

968. To what degree are the skill areas critical to team performance present?

969. What makes opportunities more or less obvious?

## 3.9 Team Member Performance Assessment: Data Communication

970. What are top priorities?

971. How accurately is your plan implemented?

972. Who they are?

973. Which training platform formats (i.e., mobile, virtual, videogame-based) were implemented in your effort(s)?

974. How effective is training that is delivered through technology-based platforms?

975. To what degree can team members frequently and easily communicate with one another?

976. What are the standards or expectations for success?

977. How are training activities developed from a technical perspective?

978. What changes do you need to make to align practices with beliefs?

979. What are the evaluation strategies (e.g., reaction, learning, behavior, results) used. What evaluation results did you have?

980. How do you use data to inform instruction and

improve staff achievement?

981. How do you make use of research?

982. What happens if a team member receives a Rating of Unsatisfactory?

983. Does platform-specific assessment information contribute to training placement or tailoring of instruction (e.g. aptitude-treatment interaction)?

984. Who receives a benchmark visit?

985. What tools are available to determine whether all contract functional and compliance areas of performance objectives, measures, and incentives have been met?

986. How is your organizations Strategic Management System tied to performance measurement?

987. To what degree does the team possess adequate membership to achieve its ends?

988. How is assessment information achieved, stored?

989. What types of learning are targeted (e.g., cognitive, affective, psychomotor, procedural)?

## 3.10 Issue Log: Data Communication

990. Is access to the Issue Log controlled?

991. Who reported the issue?

992. Who is involved as you identify stakeholders?

993. How do you manage communications?

994. What is a change?

995. What are the typical contents?

996. Are they needed?

997. Why not more evaluators?

998. Can you think of other people who might have concerns or interests?

999. How were past initiatives successful?

1000. What is the stakeholders level of authority?

1001. What is the status of the issue?

1002. Is the issue log kept in a safe place?

1003. How is this initiative related to other portfolios, programs, or Data Communication projects?

# 4.0 Monitoring and Controlling Process Group: Data Communication

1004. Do clients benefit (change) from the services?

1005. How are you doing?

1006. What departments are involved in its daily operation?

1007. What do they need to know about the Data Communication project?

1008. Are the necessary foundations in place to ensure the sustainability of the results of the programme?

1009. How can you monitor progress?

1010. Is there adequate validation on required fields?

1011. What is the expected monetary value of the Data Communication project?

1012. How well did the chosen processes fit the needs of the Data Communication project?

1013. Did you implement the program as designed?

1014. Are the services being delivered?

1015. What resources are necessary?

1016. Who are the Data Communication project stakeholders?

1017. Where is the Risk in the Data Communication project?

1018. Did it work?

1019. What input will you be required to provide the Data Communication project team?

1020. How to ensure validity, quality and consistency?

## 4.1 Project Performance Report: Data Communication

1021. How is the data used?

1022. To what degree are the tasks requirements reflected in the flow and storage of information?

1023. Next Steps?

1024. To what degree does the teams approach to its work allow for modification and improvement over time?

1025. To what degree does the formal organization make use of individual resources and meet individual needs?

1026. How will procurement be coordinated with other Data Communication project aspects, such as scheduling and performance reporting?

1027. To what degree will new and supplemental skills be introduced as the need is recognized?

1028. To what degree are the teams goals and objectives clear, simple, and measurable?

1029. To what degree do team members agree with the goals, relative importance, and the ways in which achievement will be measured?

1030. To what degree do the goals specify concrete

team work products?

1031. To what degree will team members, individually and collectively, commit time to help themselves and others learn and develop skills?

1032. To what degree is the information network consistent with the structure of the formal organization?

1033. To what degree are the goals realistic?

1034. To what degree are the members clear on what they are individually responsible for and what they are jointly responsible for?

1035. To what degree are the demands of the task compatible with and converge with the relationships of the informal organization?

1036. To what degree do the structures of the formal organization motivate taskrelevant behavior and facilitate task completion?

1037. What is the PRS?

## 4.2 Variance Analysis: Data Communication

1038. How have the setting and use of standards changed over time?

1039. What is your organizations rationale for sharing expenses and services between business segments?

1040. Are the requirements for all items of overhead established by rational, traceable processes?

1041. Are detailed work packages planned as far in advance as practicable?

1042. What is the total budget for the Data Communication project (including estimates for authorized and unpriced work)?

1043. Do the rates and prices remain constant throughout the year?

1044. What is the performance to date and material commitment?

1045. How are variances affected by multiple material and labor categories?

1046. Are control accounts opened and closed based on the start and completion of work contained therein?

1047. Are there changes in the direct base to which

overhead costs are allocated?

1048. Are the actual costs used for variance analysis reconcilable with data from the accounting system?

1049. Are the wbs and organizational levels for application of the Data Communication projected overhead costs identified?

1050. Are overhead costs budgets established on a basis consistent with the anticipated direct business base?

1051. How does your organization measure performance?

1052. Did an existing competitor change strategy?

1053. What causes selling price variance?

## 4.3 Earned Value Status: Data Communication

1054. Earned value can be used in almost any Data Communication project situation and in almost any Data Communication project environment. it may be used on large Data Communication projects, medium sized Data Communication projects, tiny Data Communication projects (in cut-down form), complex and simple Data Communication projects and in any market sector. some people, of course, know all about earned value, they have used it for years - but perhaps not as effectively as they could have?

1055. What is the unit of forecast value?

1056. Verification is a process of ensuring that the developed system satisfies the stakeholders agreements and specifications; Are you building the product right? What do you verify?

1057. How much is it going to cost by the finish?

1058. Are you hitting your Data Communication projects targets?

1059. When is it going to finish?

1060. How does this compare with other Data Communication projects?

1061. Validation is a process of ensuring that the developed system will actually achieve the stakeholders desired outcomes; Are you building the right product? What do you validate?

1062. Where are your problem areas?

1063. If earned value management (EVM) is so good in determining the true status of a Data Communication project and Data Communication project its completion, why is it that hardly any one uses it in information systems related Data Communication projects?

1064. Where is evidence-based earned value in your organization reported?

## 4.4 Risk Audit: Data Communication

1065. Do you have a realistic budget and do you present regular financial reports that identify how you are going against that budget?

1066. What resources are needed to achieve program results?

1067. What are risks and how do you manage them?

1068. How will you maximise opportunities?

1069. Does your auditor understand your business?

1070. Does the customer understand the process?

1071. What are the costs associated with late delivery or a defective product?

1072. Are procedures in place to ensure the security of staff and information and compliance with privacy legislation if applicable?

1073. What can be measured?

1074. Do the people have the right combinations of skills?

1075. Is your organization an exempt employer for payroll tax purposes?

1076. If applicable; which route/packaging option do you choose for transport of hazmat material?

1077. Do you ensure the recommended rules of play and protocols are followed for your activity?

1078. To what extent are auditors influenced by the business risk assessment in the audit process, and how can auditors create more effective mental models to more fully examine contradictory evidence?

1079. Does your organization have or has considered the need for insurance covers: public liability, professional indemnity and directors and officers liability?

1080. Are end-users enthusiastically committed to the Data Communication project and the system/product to be built?

1081. Do industry specialists and business risk auditors enhance audit reporting accuracy?

1082. Does willful intent modify risk-based auditing?

1083. The halo effect in business risk audits: can strategic risk assessment bias auditor judgment about accounting details?

## 4.5 Contractor Status Report: Data Communication

1084. Who can list a Data Communication project as organization experience, your organization or a previous employee of your organization?

1085. What was the actual budget or estimated cost for your organizations services?

1086. How is risk transferred?

1087. What was the overall budget or estimated cost?

1088. Are there contractual transfer concerns?

1089. What was the final actual cost?

1090. What was the budget or estimated cost for your organizations services?

1091. What is the average response time for answering a support call?

1092. Describe how often regular updates are made to the proposed solution. Are corresponding regular updates included in the standard maintenance plan?

1093. If applicable; describe your standard schedule for new software version releases. Are new software version releases included in the standard maintenance plan?

1094. What are the minimum and optimal bandwidth requirements for the proposed solution?

1095. What process manages the contracts?

1096. How long have you been using the services?

# 4.6 Formal Acceptance: Data Communication

1097. Did the Data Communication project manager and team act in a professional and ethical manner?

1098. Have all comments been addressed?

1099. What features, practices, and processes proved to be strengths or weaknesses?

1100. Was the client satisfied with the Data Communication project results?

1101. Do you buy pre-configured systems or build your own configuration?

1102. Do you perform formal acceptance or burn-in tests?

1103. What function(s) does it fill or meet?

1104. Do you buy-in installation services?

1105. Is formal acceptance of the Data Communication project product documented and distributed?

1106. Who supplies data?

1107. What are the requirements against which to test, Who will execute?

1108. What lessons were learned about your Data Communication project management methodology?

1109. Was the Data Communication project work done on time, within budget, and according to specification?

1110. How does your team plan to obtain formal acceptance on your Data Communication project?

1111. Does it do what client said it would?

1112. Was the Data Communication project managed well?

1113. General estimate of the costs and times to complete the Data Communication project?

1114. Who would use it?

1115. What was done right?

1116. Does it do what Data Communication project team said it would?

## 5.0 Closing Process Group: Data Communication

1117. Were the outcomes different from the already stated planned?

1118. Is there a clear cause and effect between the activity and the lesson learned?

1119. What were the actual outcomes?

1120. How will staff learn how to use the deliverables?

1121. What were things that you did very well and want to do the same again on the next Data Communication project?

1122. Did you do things well?

1123. What is the Data Communication project Management Process?

1124. Just how important is your work to the overall success of the Data Communication project?

1125. Can the lesson learned be replicated?

1126. What could be done to improve the process?

1127. What areas were overlooked on this Data Communication project?

1128. How dependent is the Data Communication

project on other Data Communication projects or work efforts?

1129. Are there funding or time constraints?

1130. Did the Data Communication project team have the right skills?

1131. Were decisions made in a timely manner?

1132. Was the user/client satisfied with the end product?

## 5.1 Procurement Audit: Data Communication

1133. Which are necessary components of a financial audit report under the Single Audit Act?

1134. Is there no evidence of any individual on the evaluation panel being biased?

1135. Does the procurement function/unit have the ability to apply public procurement principles and to prepare tender and contract documents?

1136. Is the relationship between in-house and external work considered in the strategy?

1137. Are all claims certified by the officer giving rise to the claim (usually the purchasing agent)?

1138. Are the number of checking accounts where cash segregation is not required kept to a reasonable number?

1139. When performance conditions were detailed in the tender documentation, did the contracting authority verify if the tenders received met the already stated requirements?

1140. Is the opportunity properly published?

1141. Were additional deliveries a partial replacement for normal supplies or installations or an extension of existing supplies or installations?

1142. Is your organization transparent about winning bids and prices?

1143. Are risks in the external environment identified, for example: Budgetary constraints?

1144. Does your organization use existing contracts where possible to avoid the cost of bidding?

1145. Does the procurement function/unit understand costumer needs, supply markets and suppliers?

1146. Does the contract meet criteria of completeness and consistency?

1147. Is a cash flow chart prepared and used in determining the timing and term of investments?

1148. Is there a procedure on requesting bids?

1149. Are there procedures governing the negotiations of long-term contracts?

1150. Is there management monitoring of transactions and balances?

1151. Did the chosen procedure ensure competition and transparency?

1152. Were any additional works or deliveries admissible without the need for a new procurement procedure?

## 5.2 Contract Close-Out: Data Communication

1153. Parties: who is involved?

1154. Was the contract complete without requiring numerous changes and revisions?

1155. Was the contract type appropriate?

1156. How does it work?

1157. Has each contract been audited to verify acceptance and delivery?

1158. Have all contracts been completed?

1159. How/when used ?

1160. Have all acceptance criteria been met prior to final payment to contractors?

1161. Change in attitude or behavior?

1162. Change in circumstances?

1163. Parties: Authorized?

1164. Have all contract records been included in the Data Communication project archives?

1165. Have all contracts been closed?

1166. How is the contracting office notified of the automatic contract close-out?

1167. Change in knowledge?

1168. Are the signers the authorized officials?

1169. What happens to the recipient of services?

1170. Was the contract sufficiently clear so as not to result in numerous disputes and misunderstandings?

1171. What is capture management?

## 5.3 Project or Phase Close-Out: Data Communication

1172. Who are the Data Communication project stakeholders and what are roles and involvement?

1173. What process was planned for managing issues/ risks?

1174. How often did each stakeholder need an update?

1175. Planned completion date?

1176. What are the informational communication needs for each stakeholder?

1177. Complete yes or no?

1178. Were cost budgets met?

1179. Were messages directly related to the release strategy or phases of the Data Communication project?

1180. What is the information level of detail required for each stakeholder?

1181. In preparing the Lessons Learned report, should it reflect a consensus viewpoint, or should the report reflect the different individual viewpoints?

1182. What were the desired outcomes?

1183. What is this stakeholder expecting?

1184. Did the Data Communication project management methodology work?

1185. When and how were information needs best met?

1186. What benefits or impacts does the stakeholder group expect to obtain as a result of the Data Communication project?

1187. What was expected from each stakeholder?

1188. In addition to assessing whether the Data Communication project was successful, it is equally critical to analyze why it was or was not fully successful. Are you including this?

1189. What are they?

## 5.4 Lessons Learned: Data Communication

1190. What worked well/did not work well?

1191. Which estimation issues did you personally have and what was the impact?

1192. Would you spend your own money to fix this issue?

1193. What is your overall assessment of the outcome of this Data Communication project?

1194. How was the quality of products/processes assured?

1195. How efficient and effective were Data Communication project team meetings?

1196. How useful do individuals find communications?

1197. What worked well?

1198. What is the growth stage of your organization?

1199. What are the performance measures?

1200. What is the proportion of in-house and contractor personnel authorized for the Data Communication project?

1201. What is the skill mix defined for the staffing?

1202. How clearly defined were the objectives for this Data Communication project?

1203. How was the political and social history changed over the life of the Data Communication project?

1204. What is the impact of tax policy on the case?

1205. What is the value of the deliverable?

1206. What was the single greatest success and the single greatest shortcoming or challenge from the Data Communication projects perspective?

1207. What is the fiscal dependency?

1208. Did the delivered product meet the specified requirements and goals of the Data Communication project?

# Index

Made in the USA
Las Vegas, NV
22 November 2025

34938916R00177